FROM ALLY
TO ALL-IN

amplify
an imprint of Amplify Publishing Group

www.amplifypublishinggroup.com

From Ally to All-In: The Five Stages of Moving Beyond Privilege and Becoming a More Inclusive Leader

For more information, please contact:
Amplify Publishing, an imprint of Amplify Publishing Group
620 Herndon Parkway, Suite 220
Herndon, VA 20170
info@amplifypublishing.com

Library of Congress Control Number: 2025908423

CPSIA Code: PRV0525A

ISBN-13: 979-8-89138-565-8

Printed in United States

To Kylie and Cameron—your passion for justice, fairness, and inclusion inspires me every day.

MIKE LYNCH

FROM
ALLY
TO
ALL-IN

The Five Stages of Moving Beyond Privilege
and Becoming a More Inclusive Leader

amplify

an imprint of Amplify Publishing Group

Contents

A Note for Straight White Male Leaders   ix

A Note for Leaders Representing
Historically Marginalized Communities   xiii

INTRODUCTION
Moving Beyond Allyship   xvii

CHAPTER 1
Shifting Expectations, High Stakes:
White Male Culture in DEI   1

CHAPTER 2
A Necessary Evolution: Correcting the
Course for Inclusive, Sustainable Change   13

CHAPTER 3
The Ally to All-In Framework   31

CHAPTER 4—Awareness
Opening Our Eyes: The First
Step Toward Inclusion   43

CHAPTER 5—Acknowledgment
Facing the Truth: Owning Our Role
in the System   59

CHAPTER 6—Atonement
Making Amends: Taking Responsibility
for Past Harms   75

CHAPTER 7—Accountability
Walking the Walk: Holding Ourselves
to Higher Standards   93

CHAPTER 8—Amplification
Lifting Others: Using Privilege to Empower and Advocate   **109**

CHAPTER 9
Why All-In Matters   **123**

A Final Note on the Path Forward   **137**

APPENDIX A
Self-Assessment Guide for the Ally to All-In Framework   **141**

APPENDIX B
360° Assessment Tool for the Ally to All-In Framework   **151**

APPENDIX C
Going All-In on Inclusive Leadership: A Leader's Cheat Sheet   **161**

Notes   **165**

Acknowledgments   **171**

About the Author   **173**

A NOTE FOR STRAIGHT WHITE MALE LEADERS

Take a deep breath—you've got this! First and foremost, I applaud you for your willingness to step into this diversity, equity, and inclusion (DEI) space and for striving to become a more inclusive leader. This journey is not easy, and the fact that you're here, ready to learn and grow, speaks volumes about your commitment. As you read through this book, I encourage you to "notice what you notice." This is the advice I offer all my clients in this work. Pay close attention to what stirs inside you—be it frustration, shame, pride, embarrassment, defensiveness, or hope. These emotions are your guides, each offering valuable insights into what may be triggering, affirming, or soothing for you. Recognizing these feelings is an essential part of the process, providing clues about where you are in your journey toward becoming a more inclusive leader.

I also want to address something that may come up as you navigate this content: the concept of white male privilege. For many white men, even hearing the word "privilege" can feel triggering or uncomfortable. It's important to recognize that when we talk about privilege, it doesn't mean you haven't worked hard or earned your accomplishments. You have. But the reality is, as white men, we do have an unearned advantage based on our gender and skin tone. The world at large is more suited to our advantage and, in many ways, has been built in our image.

This is often a phenomenon we don't even recognize because we're in the middle of it—much like the goldfish swimming in its own water. We don't always see the systems that are designed to support us because they've always been part of our experience. Acknowledging this privilege is not about guilt; it's about understanding the context in which we operate and using that understanding to engage more fully with others who have not had the same advantages.

This work is challenging and can be conveniently avoided, but I urge you to lean into it. We, as white men, have a unique role to play in this conversation. Even with the knowledge that we live in a world shaped largely in our likeness, we are not thriving as we might expect. In fact, there are signs that we are struggling, and the statistics are telling:

- White men report daily feelings of anxiety and depression more than non-white men.[1]
- Our enrollment and graduation rates in college are lower compared to other groups.
- We face significant declines in marriage rates and higher divorce rates, which can lead to economic and emotional stress.

- Many of us face challenges in fatherhood, including custody battles, child support issues, and maintaining relationships with our children post-divorce.
- Our life expectancy and mental health have been declining for various reasons, including:
    » An outsized impact from the opioid crisis, particularly in rural and working-class communities.
    » High rates of suicide, with 69 percent of Americans who died by suicide in 2020 being white males.[2]
    » The troubling reality that a significant number of mass shooters are white males.[3,4]

In my executive coaching experience, I can tell you anecdotally that many white men—those who most people would describe as being wildly successful—privately confess that:

- They aren't particularly happy or fulfilled.
- They have a healthy dose of imposter syndrome.
- They lack deep friendships and connections.
- A great many report that their relationships on all fronts are shaky.
- They're anguished by the fact that fulfilling their professional roles means missing out on time with their families.

These facts paint a picture of a group that is in need of change, growth, and healing. We as white men have a massive opportunity to show up differently in these DEI conversations—not just for the benefit of others, but for ourselves as well. We need what is on the other side of this journey: a healthier, more connected, and inclusive existence.

Pace yourself, take time to reflect, discuss, practice, and, above all, remain open. This journey is not about perfection but progress. It's about becoming the kind of leader who can engage deeply with others and who is open to change, even when it's difficult.

So, keep going. When it feels tough or triggering, when the emotions run high, remember that this work is vital. It's not just about making the world a better place for others; it's about improving our own lives, our relationships, and our communities. By engaging deeply and authentically, we have the potential not only to lead more inclusively but to also find a sense of purpose and well-being that has been eluding us.

A NOTE FOR LEADERS REPRESENTING HISTORICALLY MARGINALIZED COMMUNITIES

First and foremost, I want to express my deep appreciation for the path you have walked and continue to walk each day. The journey toward a more inclusive and equitable world has often placed a disproportionate burden on individuals like you—those who have had to navigate systems not designed with your success in mind. This book is a call to action for my fellow white men, but it is written with profound respect for your resilience, insight, and the invaluable contributions you bring to this work.

As you read this book, I invite you to engage with it in a way that feels right for you. You may encounter moments of affirmation, frustration, hope, or even skepticism. All of these responses are valid. This book aims to bring more white men into the conversation on DEI, urging them to go beyond surface-level allyship to deep, meaningful involvement. It acknowledges that, while the world has often centered on their experiences, it has also, paradoxically, led to struggles that many white men have yet to fully recognize or address.

Building a truly inclusive and equitable environment means understanding the challenges faced by all groups, including those who may traditionally hold privilege and power. By recognizing the struggles some white men are navigating, we can uncover opportunities to foster empathy, build bridges, and engage more leaders in the work of advancing inclusion. The reality is that white men are grappling with many challenges of their own and often face them in isolation:

- They report daily feelings of anxiety and depression more than non-white men.[1]
- Their enrollment and graduation rates in college are declining.
- They face significant rates of divorce and economic and emotional stress.
- Many struggle with the demands of fatherhood and maintaining relationships post-divorce.
- Life expectancy for white men has been on the decline, due in part to the opioid crisis, high rates of suicide, and other complex societal factors.[2]

In my executive coaching experience, I can tell you anecdotally that many white men—those who most people would describe as being wildly successful—privately confess that:

- They aren't particularly happy or fulfilled.
- They have a healthy dose of imposter syndrome.
- They lack deep friendships and connections.

- A great many report that their relationships on all fronts are shaky.
- They're anguished that fulfilling their professional roles means missing out on time with their families.

This message is not meant to center the pain of some white men above anyone else's but rather to illustrate that the systems of privilege that have historically benefited them are also failing them in critical ways. Recognizing this reality serves as an entry point for their engagement in this work, not as saviors, but as partners in a shared journey toward collective well-being.

These realities do not diminish the lived experiences of women and people of color. If anything, they highlight how systems of privilege can both harm and protect at the same time. White men benefit from an unearned advantage based on gender and skin tone, and yet, the very system that offers them these advantages can also be detrimental in other ways.

I recognize that you may have long understood the dynamics of privilege, having navigated them yourself, often from the outside looking in. As white men grapple with their own experiences of privilege, I hope this book serves as an opportunity for them to listen more closely, learn more deeply, and ultimately contribute to a more equitable world.

Pace yourself, take time to reflect, discuss, practice, and, above all, remain open to the fact that change can happen. I also encourage you to share this book with your white male colleagues, both professionally and personally. Your voices and experiences are powerful catalysts for change, and your engagement in this dialogue will make a tremendous impact.

My hope is that, as white men explore the realities of their own experiences, they will become more aware of the complexities of privilege and oppression, and how these intersect with the experiences of others. This journey is about them learning to show up differently—not just for themselves, but for you, for all of us.

I recognize that you may have been doing this work for a long time, often without the luxury of choice. You may be wondering why it has taken so long for some to even begin this journey. You may also question whether this effort will truly lead to meaningful change. These are important questions, and your perspective is essential in holding this work accountable.

Thank you for the work you've already done, often in the face of great resistance. I hope this book can serve as a bridge, bringing more people into the conversation, and ultimately leading to actions that support a more just and inclusive future for everyone.

MOVING BEYOND ALLYSHIP

In my mind, I was a staunch ally—someone who stood up for diversity, equity, and inclusion. I attended the occasional diversity meeting or event, but only when it conveniently fit into my schedule. I'd nod along, passively absorbing the discussions, but when it came time to speak up, I found myself prioritizing my own voice, eager to make my point before relinquishing the mic to others.

On social media, I'd scroll through posts about social justice issues, offering a "like" here and there, but rarely did I feel compelled to share or repost, hesitant to rock the boat or risk alienating my friends or followers. And when it came to making small changes, like using an accessible font or supporting gender-neutral bathrooms or admonishing sexist remarks, I found myself hesitating, clinging to my preferences and comfort zones rather than embracing the needs of others. I bought the books, eager to educate myself, but they ended up gathering dust on my nightstand, their chapters left unopened and unexplored. I supported political candidates who championed equality, but I mostly kept my opinions to myself, unwilling to engage in uncomfortable conversations or risk confrontation. I chose to stay silent even as I saw the rights and opportunities available to my daughters being threatened. I looked the other way as once-championed DEI efforts and initiatives were being deprioritized and dismantled.

But as I reflect on my actions over the last several years, I realize that perhaps I was only scratching the surface, content with the illusion of allyship rather than embracing the uncomfortable truths that lay beneath. When faced with challenging conversations or situations, I told myself I was being an ally, but in truth, I was calculating the risks, weighing the potential consequences of speaking out or challenging the status quo. And though I listened intently to the experiences of others, I stopped short of truly understanding, failing to empathize with their struggles or acknowledge my own complicity.

It wasn't until recently that I came to a sobering realization: I had been complacent. I had been complicit in perpetuating systems of inequality, content to stand on the sidelines rather than actively challenging the injustices that surrounded me. But now, I refuse to remain silent. I refuse to settle for the illusion of allyship. I am committed to doing the hard work—the uncomfortable work—of truly going All-In, not just in words, but in actions. It's a journey fraught with challenges and discomfort, but it's a journey that I am determined to embark upon. Because I know that true advocacy requires more than just good intentions—it requires courage, humility, vulnerability, and a willingness to confront the uncomfortable truths that lie beneath the surface.

From Ally to All-In is not political; it is not about pushing any sort of ideology, nor is it intended to shame white men. This work is not meant to be divisive. In fact, it seeks to bring us together by fostering greater understanding, conversation, and connection. We must be able to hold two truths at once: systemic advantages exist for some, and personal effort and merit also play a role in success. This journey is about expanding our perspectives and building bridges, not diminishing anyone's contributions.

I was both challenged and encouraged by my fellow DEI practitioners to write this book as they rightfully highlighted the notable absence of the white male perspective in DEI conversations. My goal is not only to offer that perspective but also to urge fellow white men to join me in this vital dialogue. I hope this book provides a deeper understanding of how white men engage—or fail to engage—in these critical discussions and offers practical tips to advance the conversation.

And so, I take a deep breath, steeling myself for the road ahead. I may stumble, I may falter, but I refuse to remain complacent. I refuse to settle for simple allyship. I want to go All-In—for myself, for those around me, and for the world at large.

I hope that you will join me on this journey.

Chapter 1

SHIFTING EXPECTATIONS, HIGH STAKES: WHITE MALE CULTURE IN DEI

"Privilege is not in and of itself bad; what matters is what we do with privilege. Privilege should be used to lift others up, not to keep them down."

BISHOP DESMOND TUTU

An Uncomfortable Ovation

In the fall of 2023, I was approached with an opportunity to speak at a DEI networking conference. The organizer called my perspective as a white cisgender heterosexual man working in the DEI space unique and he said that my presentation could fill an existing hole in the agenda. It was a sentiment I had heard often since starting my consulting business, and I was happy to participate. But I agreed to do so under the condition that I could attend the entire event. I didn't want to just go, deliver a speech, and leave. I wanted to take part in the whole experience and interact with the other attendees, which the organizer allowed and encouraged me to do.

Looking around the room on the first day of the conference, I was not surprised to be the only white man there. I had been in enough DEI environments to know that white men rarely attend. There were numerous white women there, but as the only male, the discomfort of being "the only" made me a bit hesitant about finding my lane. With this small discomfort, I could only begin to imagine how many people of color have felt working as "the only" in their fields—sometimes for years—navigating environments where they lacked the comfort of representation and shared experiences. As I participated in the group sessions and conversations, I could feel the discomfort and tension as other participants cautiously chose their words due to my presence. There was this "how is the white guy going to react to this?" look that would reverberate around the room, prompting me to chime in with, "I understand. Please don't censor yourselves on my behalf." The speakers and sessions of the conference were informative, timely, and inspiring. I learned so much, but it did contribute to my nervousness about leading my own session on the second day of the conference. I did my best to put it out of my mind though and tried to fully engage in what turned out to be a much-needed restorative experience.

Many of the professionals in attendance expressed that they had faced criticism from within their organizations for various reasons, including a lack of demonstrative results or unclear strategies, along with broader societal claims about workplaces being over-saturated by DEI. A lot of the attendees also expressed feelings of exhaustion and frustration, which inspired collaborative conversations with a focus on taking care of one another in such a demanding space to work.

On the afternoon of day two, my turn came to lead a session. I had prepared notes on how to become a more inclusive leader, and as I stood in the back of the room shuffling my note cards, I also found myself shuffling my nerves. In his brief introduction, the organizer told the crowd that I was a former HR executive who had recently branched out on my own to start a consulting firm. There was nothing necessarily special about his description of me. In fact, it was similar in nature to the various introductions I had heard him give numerous times throughout the conference. So, imagine my surprise when my walk up to the front of the room was met with an increasing round of applause that eventually turned into a cheering standing ovation. Having never experienced anything like that before, I was initially stunned by the response and thought, "Wow! How great am I?" Admittedly, the applause stroked my ego a bit, which I desperately needed in those nervous moments before my speech. I'd spent the last hour contemplating how I could use my talk to prove my worth as the only white man in attendance. I wanted the audience to feel my commitment to pursuing equity and recognize me as more than an ally. I wanted the audience to see me as All-In on this conversation. I expected a cordial applause, with a little bit of hesitance mixed in, but the thought of people getting to their feet never crossed my mind. It was a pleasant surprise that made me feel like a welcome voice.

But once my ego settled down, the discomfort of the moment hit me like a bolt of lightning with questions flooding into my mind. Why are the attendees clapping and whooping? Why are they giving me a standing ovation when all I have done so far is walk to the front of the room? What just happened? Something inside told me to pause and take in the moment. To see the bigger picture that was unfolding and invite the audience to examine it with me. I put my note cards down and after motioning for everyone to have a seat, I asked the participants if we could pivot the conversation away from my planned remarks.

"I'm curious," I said to the audience. "What just happened? While that felt great, what was that about? I had not even opened my mouth yet or provided any content, however you greeted me with such energy and enthusiasm. Tell me more." I then got quiet and listened.

The responses came quickly and openly, which mirrored the energy of the overall conference. I heard things like, "We just don't see white men participating in these conversations," and "White men are usually unwilling to engage in discussions around DEI." They also expressed a concern that, once white men do come to the table, the intention often feels performative and ingenuine. The participants gave me an appreciation for my willingness to engage and to face the discomfort of being the only white man in the room.

As we continued the dialogue, I revealed my initial uncertainties about being present at the conference, given that I was early in my journey of claiming my own space as a DEI professional and as a white man in the minority. We shared a laugh about the side eyes that I received early on in the conference. I learned that the appreciative round of applause came from my engagement in the other sessions. For networking with the other participants. For my willingness to be the "only." For being an ally. Admittedly, engaging over that day and a half was not always easy, but it ended up being exactly what the other attendees needed to see from me.

We went on to have a productive dialogue, but I still felt it was necessary to further dive into the expectations, or lack thereof, that drove the applause. There had been many great speakers during the conference, all of which happened to be Black. And some of them received standing ovations as well. But their ovations came after their speeches. In my mind, their ovations, unlike mine, had been earned. I moved the session into a conversation about the low bar that exists in the DEI space for white men, explaining to them that, in my opinion, just showing up is not enough and encouraged them to raise their expectations.

After finishing our talk, I received another round of applause along with a lot of introductions and requests to further connect. I recall how one woman expressed her appreciation, telling me that she enjoyed my session and that it was not at all what she expected to hear from me. Another person told me that, based on our conversation, he was going to intentionally engage with white male leaders in his organization on this topic. I felt that we were all leaving the session more connected and enriched by what we had learned from one another. It was an extremely productive conversation. "But," I thought to myself, "it could have been even more productive had there been other people that look like me present. It could have been so much more enriching for everyone."

I am always very clear that I only represent the perspective of one white man. I cannot and will never attempt to speak for an entire demographic of people. But I also recognize that there are some commonalities among the majority of white men that drive our unwillingness to be vulnerable in these types of conversations. The barrier to entry into this conversation is too low to be used as a reasonable excuse—we can all show up—but then what do we do once we show up? How do we engage? How do we go All-In?

Unpacking White Male Culture: Overcoming Low DEI Expectations

In recent years, I have become curious about the notion of straight white male culture and why we as a society don't talk about it more.

Even writing this now, it feels taboo to acknowledge that this is even a thing. I realize that many other groups have been discussing straight white male culture for a long time, but for many of us—and perhaps for some readers—it still feels uncomfortable and even risky to bring it up, especially in discussion with one another. I would imagine it is because our entire society and governing systems are made in the image of white men and most are not aware that this culture even exists. In the book *Inclusive Leadership: Transforming Diverse Lives, Workplaces, and Societies,* Michael Welp and Edgar H. Schein wrote a chapter entitled, "The Role of White Male Culture in Engaging White Men to be Inclusive Leaders," where they discuss how many diversity and inclusion efforts fail to engage white men effectively, often either ignoring them or casting them as the problem which "creates apathy, anger, and resentment" among this group.[1]

When I talk about white male culture, I am aware that, for many people, white supremacy is the immediate go-to association. While they are connected, it's important to distinguish the two: white male culture refers to the set of unspoken norms, behaviors, and values often centered around whiteness and masculinity that dominate many workplaces and institutions. White supremacy, on the other hand, refers to a belief system that upholds white people as inherently superior to others and justifies systems of racial oppression. While white male culture doesn't inherently advocate for oppression, it can unintentionally perpetuate inequities by centering and normalizing one perspective above others.

White supremacy is not something I can divorce myself from in terms of my physical attributes because the people who subscribe to that way of thinking look like I do. While the vast majority of white men are not in that camp, many of us do have some blind spots that contribute to the systems that were founded in white supremacy. Welp and Schein emphasize that, "White men are not focused on or examined, leading them to think diversity is not about them, and to think diversity is about helping other people with their issues."[2] This perception highlights the need for deeper engagement and self-awareness among white men regarding their role in systemic inequalities. We often cannot see enough outside of ourselves to even notice the everyday experiences of racism, inequities, and oppression that people around us experience on a daily basis.

Until the racial justice movement of 2020, we did not have to even acknowledge these societal problems. Even now, we remain comfortable in our ability to dabble in the DEI space as an item on the agenda, but our ultimate privilege is being able to easily and conveniently move on to the next thing on the list.

I recall consulting with a client who was working on DEI initiatives within an organization where she was given a new executive sponsor for this work. During one of our calls, she voiced her frustration with the new sponsor, and when I asked her to tell me more, she revealed that the sponsor shared with her that he was only taking on the DEI sponsorship role as an opportunity to network and gain some professional exposure. The client also said that when she laid out her plan to him, the sponsor replied, "Well, I think everyone is a little tired of DEI right now." The response really upset my client. She explained to me that, as a Black woman, she does not have the luxury of getting tired of this topic. The conversation is relevant to her employee experience every single day. This is the compartmentalization that goes along with white privilege. As a white man, he was able to just move on to the next thing and make a blanket statement that all people are tired of DEI, when that could not be more false for members of marginalized communities.

Straight white male culture, regardless of geographical location, shares common themes and characteristics that are shaped by historical, social, and cultural influences. This culture often places a strong emphasis on individualism and self-reliance, instilling values of strength, independence, and assertiveness from a young age. Boys are often socialized to their emotions, reflecting a societal preference for stoicism and resilience. Growing up as one of three boys, the mantra of "toughen up" was a continual undercurrent in my household.

Camaraderie, tribalism, and solidarity are also highly valued within straight white male culture, with bonds formed through shared experiences seen as symbols of strength and unity. Whether in the workplace, on the sports field, or in other male-dominated spaces, camaraderie is often characterized by banter, competition, and a shared sense of purpose. Think about the "locker room" talk that we hear from other men when they feel that they are in a safe space. While I do not agree with the often blatant misogynistic tones, I am more disturbed by those of us who compliantly nod along and laugh instead of standing up for what's right. I think of it as the "Billy Bush" effect. Most of us could relate when we saw him laugh as a US presidential candidate talked about assaulting a woman. We've all been there and continue to be there as we pick and choose our battles of when to stand up and when to stay quiet. There is this fear of "losing your man card" or "getting kicked out of the boy's club" that keeps us quiet.

As stated by Welp and Schein, "In cultures where White men are the dominant or insider group . . . most White men do not, in fact, see themselves as a group. They see themselves as individuals."[3] This individualistic view is deeply ingrained, masking the collective influences and responsibilities that come with their societal position. This lack of group identity among white men can contribute to a lack of collective responsibility, especially in addressing systemic inequalities and actively participating in DEI initiatives.

Success and achievement are central to straight white male culture, with an expectation for men to excel in various domains of life. Whether through career advancement, academic success, or athletic prowess, the pursuit of achievement is deeply ingrained, reflecting a desire to provide for oneself and one's family while leaving a lasting legacy. Our measure of success is typically based on our work history and income whereas I would imagine that women also measure success based on the relationships and community that they surround themselves with.

There is a tendency within white male culture to compartmentalize our personal and professional lives, separating the values we hold at home from the decisions we make at work. But imagine how the conversation might shift if a group of male leaders were evaluating the professional performance and potential of their own daughters in a business setting. This compartmentalization allows us to overlook our biases, shaping decisions without fully considering their broader impact. It is this mindset—enabled by privilege—that has perpetuated systemic racism, as historical and societal systems have been designed and implemented primarily by white men who could afford to dissociate themselves from the wider consequences. As white men, we often fail to see systemic issues and systemic racism because our privilege shields us from the necessity of such perspectives.

While many strengths of white male culture can be celebrated as helping to contribute to society and business, it is not without its flaws. Critics argue that it can foster toxic masculinity—a rigid adherence to traditional gender norms that stifles emotional expression and perpetuates harmful stereotypes. There is a strong bias for action and to keep moving forward regardless of the consequences. The emphasis on individualism and self-reliance can also lead to feelings of isolation and loneliness, as men may struggle to connect with others on a deeper level. It's the "not wanting to stop and ask for directions" phenomenon where we think that we need to figure things out on our own. But that trait does not translate in the DEI space very well because there is no way that anyone can do this work all on their own. Yet the reaction I get a lot of times from leaders is, "Give me all the data, I'll analyze it and come back with a solution." Then, more often than not, they come back with a suggestion to recruit more from HBCUs. Well, we already do that, and it is not, in and of itself, the answer to DEI. Moving the conversation forward is a team sport and the arrogant belief that one person can "fix it" on their own keeps us from moving forward.

When they figure out that they cannot solve the problem, they hire a DEI expert to come in and do the work for them. Yes, bringing in an expert is useful, but you also need to play an active role in the process. Tomorrow, I can't just walk up to an organization and start a DEI conversation. First, I have to build trust with the employees.

In recent years, straight white male culture has faced increasing scrutiny as society grapples with issues of diversity, equity, and inclusion. There is a growing recognition of the need to redefine masculinity in more inclusive and equitable ways, challenging out-dated stereotypes and embracing a broader range of identities and experiences. I do not offer this perspective as an excuse for the absence of white men in important DEI conversations. I am also not trying to criticize white men, because I genuinely believe they can bring valuable strengths to this work—such as their ability to influence others, open doors for change, and use their privilege to amplify marginalized voices. But I want us to understand that there could be a reason why white men tend to behave the way that we do, especially considering the extensive amount of social program-ming that some of us have received our whole lives. But because strengths like individualism and self-reliance are so ingrained in us, we will continuously hit a wall in the DEI conversation if we don't acknowledge that some of those strengths are preventing us from getting to the other side. They keep us from reaching a place of vulnerability, keep us from reflecting and listening, which are the critical behaviors that will move these conversations forward.

Ultimately, straight white male culture is a dynamic and evolv-ing phenomenon, shaped by a complex interplay of historical, social, and cultural factors. As we navigate the complexities of contemporary society, our challenge is to first recognize that this white male culture exists and then embrace its strengths while also confronting its shortcomings, working toward a future where all individuals, regardless of race, gender, or background, can thrive and succeed.

Chapter 2

A NECESSARY EVOLUTION: CORRECTING THE COURSE FOR INCLUSIVE, SUSTAINABLE CHANGE

"Inclusion is not bringing people into what already exists; it is making a new space, a better space for everyone."

GEORGE DEI

Inclusion Beyond HR

I stumbled into my first HR job quite by accident. Post-college, before entering the corporate world, I lived an adventurous life as a ski instructor, a whitewater rafting guide, and a teacher at a boarding school. My career trajectory took a surprising turn when I secured my first HR role as a campus recruiter for a financial services company where I would end up staying for the next twenty-five years.

In that first HR role, I traveled across the country inspiring students to embark on their careers in banking. From the outset our focus was not only on attracting the best talent but also on ensuring diversity in our recruitment efforts. This aspect of the job was particularly fulfilling, as it resonated deeply with my belief in creating inclusive opportunities for all. But while DEI work was always a part of our efforts, it usually existed on the fringe, not fully integrated into the core business strategies. It often felt like we were kicking the can down the road instead of making real, sustainable progress because, prior to 2020, DEI was viewed as an option instead of an integrated priority. I can remember numerous occasions where I crafted diversity topic agendas for discussion during leadership team meetings, only to have those agenda items continuously pushed back to the next meeting, the next month, or even the next quarter. I didn't see it as an intentional disregard for diversity because there was allyship there. Conversations were happening and movements to diversify the workforce were being made. But there were no DEI strategies, task forces, or dedicated resources. Instead, the conversations centered solely on representation and getting more diverse talent. While representation is important, focusing only on it often reduces the work to optics—checking a box rather than addressing systemic barriers. DEI strategies and task forces, on the other hand, are essential for creating real, sustainable change by fostering inclusion, equity, and a culture that supports diverse talent beyond just recruitment.

When I first started working in HR, organizations rarely had specific resources or a specific person on the team who was fully dedicated to recruiting. But over time companies began hiring a person (usually a woman) to focus on diversity talent acquisition and began to create strategies to become more inclusive, which was a positive move forward. Then, the HR landscape slowly shifted until it wasn't about just having one person focusing on diversity, but every recruiter needed to include diversity goals within their overall strategy. It evolved from simply hiring ten statisticians as quickly as possible to fill a need—regardless of how diverse the representation was—to continuously recruiting until a diverse talent pool of ten statisticians was identified and hired.

Over the years, recruiting was one of the many hats I wore in my HR journey. I also took on roles such as trainer, program manager, and HR business partner for several different lines of business. Each position brought its own set of challenges and learning experiences, shaping me into a versatile HR professional. As a trainer, I developed and delivered programs that enhanced employee skills and engagement. As a program manager, I oversaw initiatives that streamlined processes and improved efficiency for development programs. As an HR business partner, I worked closely with leaders and teams to drive organizational success through strategic HR practices. Throughout these roles, DEI initiatives were present, but they continued to feel like supplementary efforts rather than central components of our mission.

Every time a DEI conversation took place, it felt like business leaders turned to me as an HR person to essentially ask, "Okay, what are you going to do about it?" While I understood where that intent came from given that DEI initiatives and HR processes are connected, I was constantly asserting that these were not strictly HR issues to solve. They were business issues to solve. And yes, HR played a critical role in that, but we also needed the business to really step up and lead in that space.

There was one position I held where the organization created a diversity council led by a Black woman on the team. When she left the company, my boss approached me about stepping in as the main HR support for the council. I had built a reputation of being able to move quickly through distractions and actually get things done. So, in my very white male confident way, I said, "Okay, give it to me. I'm going to take this on." I partnered with a white male senior executive whom I thought could help remove barriers and push the initiatives along. Though we were making an effort and doing the work, I recall feeling like it was mostly in vain and we were not making much progress. We were very methodical and focused on getting to the diversity representation numbers we needed. We wanted to make progress on our stated goals, which was important, but what we didn't have was a real gauge on whether we were contributing to the progression of meaningful diversity or getting in the way of it.

I came up with a plan—which I thought was brilliant at the time—to hold diversity council meetings every two months where I would invite, for example, a Hispanic leader or a female employee to come in and tell us about their experience within the company. These meetings essentially ran through the rainbow of diversity in the spirit of trying to give people a voice, which I think was helpful to an extent, but ultimately failed to move the needle forward. People still felt unheard, and there was little evidence of meaningful learning, change, or actionable outcomes as a result. It is with some shame that I think about it now, because we should have brought in white male leaders and asked them what they were doing or not doing in the diversity space. I fell into the trap and I didn't even know it. I thought we were doing the right thing since we did make some progress in terms of measures, reports, and tracking methodologies. Yet, it still felt a little bit like a hamster wheel in that we were trying a lot of things but weren't making any real progress. We played the role of good allies but never reached the level of going All-In. Reflecting on that time, I now know that we missed the mark by not including white men in the conversation around creating a more inclusive environment. Instead, we placed the burden on the backs of employees from historically underrepresented groups.

In 2017, I was offered an exciting opportunity to move to the UK to lead HR for an international business. This role allowed me to see HR from an end-to-end perspective and understand how to integrate HR into business decisions effectively. Alongside my role as Head of HR, I had the privilege of serving as the accountable executive for DEI.

In this capacity I championed DEI initiatives, working to bring these efforts from the periphery to the forefront of our strategic priorities. I wanted to change the perception of DEI as simply an HR concern and move it into the forefront as a general business concern. Ensuring that our strategies and practices fostered an inclusive and equitable workplace became a central and integrated goal. I worked tirelessly to promote diversity, advocate for equity, and cultivate a culture of inclusion. But along the way, the absence of white men pushing these conversations became increasingly apparent to me. These experiences not only reinforced my commitment to DEI but they also highlighted the critical importance of integrating principles and practices in order to drive organizational success.

The Missing Voice

After a twenty-five-year career as a human resources leader and executive, I found myself back in the job market exploring two potential paths: starting my own coaching and consulting business or pursuing another executive-level HR leadership role. Given my extensive experience, I was confident in my qualifications and eagerly pursued several opportunities that aligned with my skill set. I also engaged with various headhunters who echoed my optimism, consistently noting that my background and experience were a strong fit for the roles I was targeting. I believed that I had one more turn up at bat for a meaningful HR leadership role and I did not anticipate any obstacles to securing a position. Because diversity, equity, and inclusion were still very important to me, I wanted to work with an organization that aligned with my values, which I made very clear in my interviews.

However, time and again, despite my qualifications and experience, I received feedback along the lines of: "You look great and are qualified for the role, and your experience aligns with what the organization is looking for. However, we are committed to presenting a diverse slate of candidates first. Should none of those candidates be successful, we will come back around to you."

My feelings about these responses were mixed. As someone who has long been an advocate for diversity and inclusion, I understood and supported this approach, and I probably would have run my candidate search in the exact same way. Yet, understanding the rationale behind prioritizing a diverse slate of candidates did not entirely shield me from a mix of complex emotions. I decided to do my own very unscientific experiment. I asked the headhunters to follow-up with me to let me know whether the companies hired a diverse applicant, and 100 percent of the time, they had. There was not a single white man hired into those roles. And again, I'm not disagreeing with that stance. I truly believe that if there's a chance to diversify or increase representation among senior leadership, an organization should do so, but that belief did not numb the feelings of disappointment, frustration, and even a sense of unfairness. Despite my extensive qualifications, I was not being given immediate consideration due to my identity as a white male. I was a gray-haired white man in my fifties who couldn't get a job that met my expectations and leveraged my experience.

I had heard this same sentiment of unfairness from other white men with a similar story, a sentiment that I had spent years preaching against, so I knew that I couldn't accept this opinion for myself. It reinforced for me why it's so important for more white men to join the DEI conversation: by sharing their stories, they can begin to understand and empathize with the frustrations and inequities that so many others have been experiencing for years. I needed to explore this thing, which started with joining a couple of diversity forums, where I was always the only white man there. I also started researching information on white privilege, including how to reconcile and overcome it. But there was nothing. Nothing that really spoke to me as a white man about how to productively engage in this conversation. I realized that I had gotten a small glimpse into the experiences that many women and people of color have faced for years—being equally qualified, yet not considered the "first choice" due to systemic biases and judgements based on someone's appearance. For the first time, I felt a personal connection to the challenges that underrepresented groups encounter in the job market.

This realization was both humbling and enlightening. It reminded me that, while I had been an advocate for DEI, there were layers of emotion and experiences I hadn't fully grasped until I faced them myself. This journey has been a profound learning opportunity, deepening my empathy for those who have been marginalized and overlooked despite their qualifications. It reinforced my commitment to creating change and advancing the DEI conversation. I now see more clearly how critical it is to address the systemic barriers that have historically disadvantaged certain groups. My own feelings of frustration and unfairness have been a catalyst for greater understanding and a renewed dedication to advocating for inclusive hiring practices.

Once I gained that awareness, I couldn't look the other way, and the more I explored, the more I recognized that a voice was missing in the DEI space, a void that I could fill. The folks who have been carrying the load in the DEI practitioner space are really good at what they do, but I often find they are exhausted from doing the work alone without the solid partnership required to move progress along. As I talked to diversity practitioners, I heard them saying, "I can't do this work anymore. Funding is starting to get ripped out from under us." "We are frustrated by the lack of support." "I question how committed the leaders are to this work." I wanted to help bridge that gap.

After six months of headhunters, interviews, and rejections, I made the decision to take myself out of the job market. I decided to do my own thing. As a white male, I recognize the importance of using my experience and position to amplify the voices of those who have been underrepresented. I can use my platform to foster more inclusive environments, where diverse talent is not just something to consider but is actually celebrated and prioritized. This involves not only supporting policies that promote diversity but also actively mentoring and sponsoring individuals from underrepresented backgrounds. I realize that may come off as opportunistic, and that's not super inspiring, but truthfully, that is what focused my attention to furthering inclusion . . . and again, once I saw the gap left by white men, I could not unsee it. The toothpaste was out of the tube, and I wanted to help other white men get to that place of seeing because once you start to notice the macroaggressions of systemic racism, misogyny, etc., and the microaggressions that result from them, how can you look the other way? I knew for myself that I could no longer look the other way.

In sharing my story, I aim to encourage other white men to reflect on their own experiences and feelings in the evolving job market landscape. By acknowledging our emotions and understanding our roots, we can become more empathetic allies in the pursuit of equity. It's about moving from passive awareness to active engagement in creating inclusive workplaces where everyone has an equal opportunity to succeed. This journey has been a reminder that true inclusion involves understanding and addressing both the visible and invisible barriers that people face. It has shown me that the path to equity requires not just structural changes but also a personal commitment to growth and empathy. In embracing these lessons, I am more equipped than ever to contribute to a more just and inclusive future.

I believe that many white men are simply moving through life as usual, often caring about these issues but not always feeling compelled to take action. Their support often feels passive, as if staying out of the way and cheering from the sidelines is enough. However, in my work with white male leaders, I've come to understand that this isn't due to a lack of care—it's often because they don't know how to effectively engage in these conversations. They may be unsure of what to say or how to say it. DEI is an ongoing journey, and I genuinely believe that most white men are also on their own journey, capable of growing into active, wholehearted advocates who are truly All-In.

A Necessary Correction for Sustainable Change

The tragic death of George Floyd in 2020 ignited a global reckoning with issues of racial injustice and inequality, leading to a surge of commitment toward DEI across many sectors. Organizations responded with a flurry of initiatives aimed at addressing systemic biases and promoting diversity in their ranks. This wave of activity, driven by a heightened sense of urgency, often led to a wide range of actions—some well-considered, others more reactionary.

Companies and organizations, eager to demonstrate their commitment to change, implemented a variety of measures, from diversifying leadership teams to launching new training programs. While these efforts were crucial in sparking conversations and raising awareness, they were sometimes characterized by an "overswing"—a rapid, often unfocused response to a deeply complex issue. A notable aspect of this surge was the burden placed on women and people of color to lead the charge. Many of these individuals were called upon to educate, advocate, and spearhead DEI initiatives, often without adequate support or recognition. Meanwhile, many leaders, particularly white male leaders, remained passive, not fully engaging in or taking ownership of these efforts. This dynamic left much of the work to those already marginalized, rather than distributing the responsibility across all leadership levels.

As we move forward, we are witnessing what many describe as a "backlash" against these DEI efforts, often taking the form of resistance from leaders or employees who feel alienated by these initiatives, or public criticism that frames DEI as unnecessary or overly political. In some cases, it's seen in the scaling back of DEI programs and budgets or the accusation of inclusion work as divisive rather than unifying. However, it's important to frame this backlash not as a rejection of the principles of DEI. Rather, it should be viewed through the lens of reflection and necessary correction. I would reframe this as a collective pause, allowing organizations to evaluate what has been effective and what hasn't. This recalibration is essential for moving beyond symbolic gestures toward concrete, lasting change. It's a recognition that while the initial surge was necessary, it must be followed by a more thoughtful and deliberate approach. This backlash also underscores a broader societal discomfort with rapid change and a reassessment of priorities. Some view the backlash as resistance to diversity initiatives, but it can also be seen as a call for more precision and focus on how DEI goals are set and pursued. Importantly, this period offers a crucial opportunity to correct the oversight of sidelining certain leaders and to encourage more inclusive participation in DEI efforts.

In this correction phase, there is an imperative to not only continue DEI efforts but to widen the range of those who are actively involved. I would argue that this includes a specific call to action for white male leaders, who have often been left "off the hook" and allowed to remain passive. Now is the time to invite and, indeed, demand that they join as active participants in this critical work. White male leaders must not only support DEI initiatives but also take a proactive role in advocating for and driving these efforts. They should use their influence and positions of power to champion diversity, challenge systemic inequities, and ensure that DEI principles are integrated into the core strategies and values of their organizations.

Rather than retreating from DEI commitments, the current moment offers an opportunity to refine and focus our efforts. It's about shifting from a reactive to a proactive stance, where

DEI is integrated into the core strategies and values of an organization. This involves setting realistic, measurable goals, engaging in continuous learning, and creating systems of accountability that go beyond surface-level changes. A key part of this correction involves encouraging all leaders to take a more active role in advocating for DEI efforts. Leaders must not only support these initiatives but also be vocal champions for them, highlighting their importance and advocating for the resources necessary to achieve meaningful outcomes. By doing so, they set a tone that prioritizes equity and inclusion as integral to the organization's success.

It's crucial to maintain perspective during this period of correction. The progress made in the wake of 2020 should not be dismissed or undervalued. At the same time, there is a need for ongoing evaluation and adaptation. The journey toward a truly inclusive environment is long and requires sustained effort. By embracing this moment of correction, organizations can build on the foundations laid in recent years, ensuring that DEI efforts are not only impactful but also enduring. This involves a commitment to continuous improvement, openness to feedback, and a willingness to address and rectify missteps along the way.

The DEI backlash, while challenging, is a vital part of the process toward creating a more inclusive and equitable society. It is an opportunity for growth and refinement, paving the way for a more focused and effective approach to diversity and inclusion. By staying committed and adaptive, we can ensure that DEI remains a central and enduring priority, with active participation from all leaders, especially those whose allyship has been more passive than productive.

Allyship Is Just the Beginning

Allyship is an essential starting point in the journey toward a more inclusive and equitable world, but it is not the destination. Over the years I have witnessed, and at times embodied, a version of allyship that feels like an end in itself—a box checked, a badge of honor earned. Many of the white men I coach proudly declare themselves allies, as if this self-designation grants them immunity from further responsibility in the DEI space. They say things like, "I have a Black friend," or "A gay couple lives next door and we're friendly with them," or "I champion my daughter." While these statements indicate some level of awareness, they can also mask a deeper complacency. Being an ally is a good start, but it is not enough to move the needle. It feels like a convenient stopping point, a place where we can pat ourselves on the back and feel good about the work we've done without grappling with the systemic changes that are truly needed.

It's easy to see why so many white men fall into this trap. Allyship feels safe. It offers a sense of moral high ground without demanding too much risk or discomfort. You can be an ally from the sidelines—cheering for progress, applauding the efforts of others, and feeling like you're on the right side of history. It's not that these actions are wrong or unimportant; they are crucial first steps. But stopping there creates a false sense of accomplishment. It's a half-measure, a way of engaging with the work without fully confronting its demands. To be truly impactful we have to push beyond this comfort zone and dive into the messy, challenging, and often uncomfortable realities of what it means to go All-In.

I understand this firsthand because I've been there. I, too, have rested in the comfort of allyship, convincing myself that my efforts were sufficient. I would attend the meetings, say the right things, and rally for what I believed was right. Yet, I often stopped short of confronting the deeper, more uncomfortable issues head-on. There were moments when I told myself that my support was enough, that I could shift my focus elsewhere with a clear conscience. I convinced myself that I was doing enough simply by not being part of the problem of oppression. But deep down, I knew that if I, as an ally, was willing to tolerate bias and discrimination without taking direct action, then I was no better than those who perpetuate these issues. For too long I tolerated the status quo, not realizing that this tolerance was in itself a part of the problem. True change demands more than passive support. It requires active engagement, the willingness to confront and dismantle the systems of inequality we are a part of.

Even now, I fall short more times than I would like to admit. I remember a recent conversation with a Black woman where I found myself on my soapbox, telling her what I thought she needed to do. In my mind, I was offering support, sharing insights that I thought would be helpful. But she stopped me with a simple, yet powerful, reminder: "I don't need you to teach me about my own oppression." Though my intention was to help, I had to confront the reality of how I was coming across. I was centering myself in the conversation, assuming I had the answers instead of listening. In that moment, I was reminded that allyship requires humility and the ability to decenter oneself. I could have beaten myself up over the interaction, but instead, I chose to accept my mistake and commit to doing better. It is interactions like this one that are continual wake-up calls to be more open, to listen first rather than feeling the need to speak first. This is the work of moving from allyship to being All-In—learning to step back, to be a supportive presence rather than a dominating voice. This doesn't mean being passive or silent; it means actively supporting others by creating space for their voices to be heard first and amplifying their perspectives. It's about knowing when to listen and when to speak, and ensuring that when you do speak, it's to support the cause, not to center yourself.

Most white men are just going about their lives, believing they care about these issues without actually doing the hard work. We tell ourselves, "I would never get in the way. I'll support you from the sidelines." We convince ourselves that this passive support is enough, but in reality, it's a way to avoid stepping into the uncomfortable space of true action. We care, but we don't know how to care in a way that moves beyond words into transformative action. This misunderstanding stems from a lack of deeper engagement with the realities of white male culture and systemic inequality. It's easy to support DEI initiatives in theory, to agree with the broad strokes of inclusion and fairness. But when it comes to the granular, often messy work of challenging our own biases, confronting uncomfortable truths, and making sacrifices for the greater good, many of us hesitate.

My journey from ally to being All-In didn't happen overnight. It was not a sudden epiphany that spurred me to shout this message from the mountaintop. It has been, and continues to be, a deliberate, progressive, ongoing effort to push beyond the comfort of allyship into a place of active commitment. I am a work in progress, just like the majority of white men who want to do better but don't always know how. The challenge is to move from the safety of our whitewashed world—a world where all our needs are met and where it's easy to fade into the background—and make the conscious choice to engage fully. By staying in that world, we miss out on the depth of relationships, perspectives, and cultures that enrich not just others, but ourselves.

Going All-In requires us to confront not just the external barriers to inclusion but also our internal resistance. It demands that we question our assumptions, sit with our discomfort, and be willing to make mistakes—and then learn from them. It's about understanding that allyship is not a title to be claimed once and for all; it is a daily practice, a commitment to continuous growth and learning. It means using our privilege not to speak for others but to amplify their voices, to create spaces where they can speak for themselves. Reflecting on my own previously shared experience of speaking with the Black woman, I realize I could have asked her about her perspective instead of telling her about her own oppression. By listening more and centering her voice in the conversation, I could have better supported and amplified her experience rather than unintentionally overshadowing it. It comes down to being willing to take risks, to face pushbacks, and to be okay with not always being comfortable or liked.

It's vital to be clear about one thing: this is not about white men being saviors in the DEI space, nor is it about centering our experiences in these conversations. It's about catching up to the work that has already been done by those who have been fighting this fight for far longer. It's about going All-In to maintain the progress that has been made and to drive forward the ultimate goal of a truly inclusive future. It's about showing up not as heroes, but as committed partners in the ongoing struggle for equity. We need to recognize that the work is not about us, but it requires us. It requires us to move beyond the safety of allyship and into the vulnerable, courageous space of being All-In.

This transition demands an active and conscious commitment. The comfort of our whitewashed world is deceptive. By staying in that world, we make a deliberate choice to give up on all the things that could happen—the depth of relationships we could form, the different cultures and perspectives we could learn from, the growth we could experience. Being All-In means choosing to fight against that pull of comfort, to step into the unknown not because we have all the answers, but because we are committed to seeking them out.

In the end, being All-In is not about being perfect. It's about being present. It's about showing up, again and again, even when it's hard, even when it's uncomfortable. It's about recognizing that our journey doesn't have a finish line, and that our role is not to lead but to support, to listen, and to act. It's about understanding that being an ally was never meant to be a resting place but a launching pad for deeper, more transformative work. This work is not easy, and it never will be. But it is necessary, and it is worth it. And it's time we, especially white men, stop seeing allyship as the end and start embracing it as the beginning of our All-In commitment to a truly inclusive future.

Chapter 3

THE ALLY TO ALL-IN FRAMEWORK

*"Do the best you can until you know better.
Then when you know better, do better."*

MAYA ANGELOU

The Business Case for Change

Diversity, equity, and inclusion are not just buzzwords; they are essential drivers of organizational success, they foster creativity, innovation, and growth. When we talk about the impact of DEI, we are talking about how diverse teams drive creativity and innovation, enhance overall performance, improve employee engagement and retention, and contribute to market growth. The case for DEI has long been made, but it is worth repeating. Inclusion is not just ethical, it's strategic, supported by compelling data and research.

Diverse teams are found to be more creative and open to innovation, which ultimately leads to improved business performance. When individuals from varied backgrounds, experiences, and perspectives come together, they each bring unique ideas and approaches that ignite creativity. A study by Boston Consulting

Group (BCG) found that companies with more diverse management teams experience 19 percent higher revenue due to innovation.[1] This makes diversity a key ingredient for generating new ideas and staying competitive in an ever-changing market. Research by management consulting firm McKinsey & Company further emphasizes this point, revealing that ethnically diverse companies are 36 percent more likely to outperform their peers on profitability.[2] Additionally, a report from Harvard Business Review shows that diverse teams can solve problems faster than cognitively similar teams, highlighting that diversity is not just about representation—it is also about tangible results that can make or break an organization's success.[3]

The impact of diversity on organizational performance cannot be understated. Diverse leadership teams are more effective and consistently produce superior results. According to McKinsey & Company, companies in the top quartile for gender diversity on executive teams are 21 percent more likely to outperform others on profitability and 27 percent more likely to create superior value.[4] When it comes to ethnic diversity, the numbers are just as striking. Companies in the top quartile for ethnic diversity in leadership are 33 percent more likely to lead their industries in profitability.[5] These statistics underscore a fundamental truth: diverse leadership leads to better business outcomes, full stop.

Employee engagement and retention are also significantly impacted by a commitment to inclusion. When employees feel that their voices matter and their contributions are valued, they are more likely to be engaged and committed. Research from Deloitte shows that inclusive teams outperform their peers by 80 percent in team-based assessments.[6] Inclusive practices not only boost morale but also help organizations retain top talent, reducing turnover and the costs associated with it.

The benefits of diverse teams extend beyond internal success to external growth as well. Companies with diverse teams are 70 percent more likely to capture new markets, according to Harvard Business Review.[7] This advantage stems from the unique perspectives that diverse individuals bring, helping organizations better understand and serve the needs of diverse customer bases. This leads to enhanced customer orientation, higher employee satisfaction, and improved decision-making—a virtuous cycle that drives continuous growth and competitive advantage.

The impact of DEI is maximized when coupled with inclusive leadership. Leaders who pursue inclusivity play a crucial role in creating environments where diverse perspectives are welcomed and valued, driving creativity and boosting decision-making. When leaders actively foster a sense of belonging among their team members, it results in higher morale and stronger commitment. Employees are more likely to be engaged and motivated when they feel that their voices are heard and their contributions recognized. Moreover, inclusive leaders attract a broader talent pool, enhancing team versatility and adaptability, and positioning their organizations to succeed in a rapidly evolving marketplace.

When leaders consider a variety of perspectives and experiences, they make more well-rounded and informed choices, reducing the risk of bias and groupthink. By valuing diverse viewpoints, organizations become more agile, adaptive, and able to navigate complex challenges with innovative solutions.

Companies known for their commitment to inclusive practices often enjoy greater brand loyalty and trust from customers, clients, and the public. A reputation for inclusion not only attracts customers but also positions the organization as an employer of choice, enhancing its ability to attract and retain top talent through a positive work culture that reduces turnover rates. When people feel respected, supported, and included, they are more likely to stay, contributing to the organization's and shareholders' long-term success. It also positively reflects on the leader's brand, enhancing their credibility as an effective people manager.

Navigating compliance and reducing risk are additional benefits of inclusive leadership. Proactively addressing diversity issues helps organizations stay ahead of legal and regulatory requirements, mitigating the risk of lawsuits and negative publicity. It's not just about doing the right thing—it's about being strategic and proactive in mitigating risks.

Global competitiveness is another major advantage that inclusive leadership brings. In a world that is increasingly diverse and interconnected, organizations with inclusive leaders are better positioned to understand and succeed in different markets. These leaders bring cultural intelligence and a global mindset, enabling their organizations to navigate the complexities of diverse markets more effectively.

Finally, inclusive leadership fosters personal growth and learning. Exposure to different perspectives and ideas enhances leaders' cultural intelligence and their ability to lead in diverse environments. This personal growth is essential in today's world, where adaptability, empathy, and a willingness to learn are key leadership traits.

The case for inclusivity is supported by data, positive business outcomes, and the testimonies of growth it has facilitated for individuals and organizations alike. Diversity and inclusion are more than ethical imperatives—they are strategic drivers that lead to enhanced creativity, innovation, performance, and long-term success. As All-In advocates, it is our responsibility to push back against efforts to reverse progress and actively encourage the organizations we work for, and the companies whose goods and services we consume, to stay committed to their DEI efforts. Going All-In on DEI is about creating a fairer, more successful future for all of us—a future where every voice is heard, and every person has the opportunity to contribute and thrive.

The White Male Quadrant

In 2017, after nearly twenty years in human resources, I had an experience that shifted everything for me. At the time I was working in the UK as the Head of International HR and Communications for a Fortune 100 global financial services company. At this point in my career, I'd attended plenty of DEI trainings, and frankly, I thought I had a pretty good handle on the subject. But then, I was asked to fly back to the States for a multi-day, company-wide HR executive conference. What started as a typical DEI session quickly became a life and career-changing experience.

About halfway through the training we returned to the conference room after a break with snacks and light-hearted banter to find that the facilitator had set up a massive 2x2 matrix on the floor, like a four-square court. The quadrants were labeled: *White men*, *White women*, *Non-white men*, and *Non-white women*. After we all gathered around the square, the facilitator asked us to step into the quadrant we most identified with.

As you might expect in HR—a profession dominated by women—most of my colleagues stepped into the "White Women" box. A few Black and Asian women stepped into the "Non-White Women" square, while two or three of us walked over to the "White Men" box. The "Non-White Men" box remained empty.

Then came the facilitator's next instruction: "Now, step into the quadrant that has the greatest power and influence to improve the DEI landscape."

Without hesitation, everyone in the room immediately moved to the "White Men" box—my box. I was stunned, not just by the sheer speed of the migration, but by how silent and automatic it was.

In that moment, I realized something I'd never fully grasped before: there was an absolute, unspoken expectation that white men—people like me—were expected to lead in DEI efforts. And yet, no one had ever told us this. We had no idea. Despite years of working in HR, deeply understanding the business case for DEI, and genuinely believing I was an ally, the truth was that I'd been sleepwalking through DEI conversations.

That moment gave me a whole new lens to DEI. I saw how disconnected I had been from the real work of inclusion. It wasn't enough to attend trainings or voice statements of support; I had to step into a leadership role, not just because of my position or title, but because of the influence and responsibility I held as a white man.

This awakening was the seed that eventually grew into the Ally to All-In Framework. I knew that leaders, especially white men, needed more than a general awareness of inequity—we needed a roadmap, a framework to move us from passive allyship to active, ongoing engagement in DEI work. We needed a structured path to help us reflect, take accountability, and use our privilege to amplify the voices and needs of others.

This framework wasn't just about becoming better allies; it was about going All-In—understanding the unique role we play in shaping the DEI landscape and committing to leading from the front. Ally to All-In is the result of that commitment, and it's my way of ensuring that other leaders can find their way, just as I found mine.

The Framework

The Ally to All-In Framework is designed to guide individuals on a transformative journey of self-discovery and toward wholehearted commitment to diversity, equity, inclusion, accessibility, and belonging. Despite my best efforts to overcomplicate the framework with loads of academic research and theories, it was crafted with simplicity and purpose. The framework is built on the foundation of allyship or, at least, the intent of allyship. From there, the framework comprises five pivotal steps, each crafted to facilitate a profound shift in consciousness and action. These steps serve as the building blocks for leaders to evolve from passive allies to accomplices of change, igniting profound shifts in both personal and professional spheres. The destination, although aspirational and sometimes elusive, is the notion of being All-In.

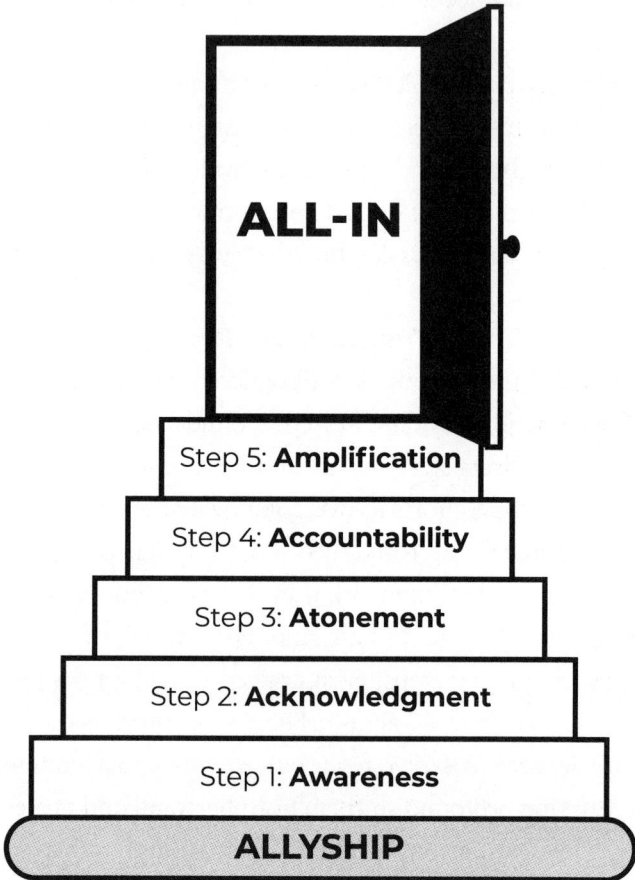

ALL-IN

Step 5: **Amplification**

Step 4: **Accountability**

Step 3: **Atonement**

Step 2: **Acknowledgment**

Step 1: **Awareness**

ALLYSHIP

Step 1: Awareness

Awareness serves as the foundational cornerstone, inviting individuals to embark on a journey of introspection and understanding. It is a call to recognize and comprehend the intricate web of privilege that permeates our workplaces and communities, shedding light on the pervasive disparities that persist. By embracing awareness, individuals lay the groundwork for informed action, confronting biases and the challenges of inequality with clarity and conviction.

Step 2: Acknowledgment

Acknowledgment marks a pivotal moment of reckoning, urging individuals to confront their own privilege and complicity in perpetuating systemic injustices. It is a courageous step toward self-awareness and accountability, as individuals come to terms with the realities of historical and current inequalities. Through acknowledgment, individuals affirm their commitment to fostering an inclusive environment, recognizing their role in shaping a more equitable world. A critical action for this step is the ability to not only voice your acknowledgment to yourself, but to others as well. This is a critical step to start building trust.

Step 3: Atonement

Atonement propels leaders into action, inspiring intentional efforts to redress past wrongs and begin the process of rectifying systemic injustices. It is a call to make amends, to actively seek ways to address the impact of privilege and inequality on marginalized communities. With humility and determination, individuals embark on a journey of restitution, striving to create a more just and equitable society for all.

Step 4: Accountability

Accountability heralds a new era of responsibility as individuals commit to upholding the principles of diversity, equity, and inclusion in all aspects of their personal and professional lives. It is a call to action, urging individuals to challenge bias, foster inclusivity, and advocate for equity in every sphere of influence. Through accountability, individuals embrace their role as agents of change, holding themselves and others responsible for creating a more just and equitable world.

Step 5: Amplification

Amplification shines a spotlight on the voices and contributions of those who have been historically marginalized, ensuring their perspectives are heard and valued. It is a commitment to elevating the stories, achievements, and concerns of underrepresented groups in all areas of life. Amplification is an active process, encouraging individuals to use their platforms and influence to highlight diverse experiences and advocate for systemic change. By amplifying these voices, individuals become powerful allies, fostering a culture of inclusivity and recognition. This journey requires dedication and collective effort, as we all have a role to play in magnifying the impact of those who have been overlooked. Amplification is also about leveraging your privilege and platform to champion change. Through amplification, we can create a more inclusive and equitable world where every voice is heard and celebrated.

Leveraging the Ally to All-In Framework

As I work with leaders to progress through the Ally to All-In Framework, I see them embark on a journey of profound transformation, deepening their engagement and commitment to the principles of DEI. Moving beyond mere allyship, leaders emerge as catalysts for change, champions of justice, and advocates for a more equitable and inclusive society. In embracing the process, individuals embark on a journey of empowerment and enlightenment, forging a path toward a brighter, more inclusive future for all.

This transformative framework has significantly enhanced the impact of my consulting business by empowering leaders to actively engage in DEI conversations and foster a culture of inclusivity. By adopting this model, leaders can move beyond passive support and become proactive champions of DEI initiatives. They gain the necessary insights and strategies to navigate complex discussions effectively. As leaders become more adept and confident at addressing DEI issues, they foster an environment where all employees feel valued and heard, leading to higher engagement and morale.

The Ally to All-In Framework establishes a shared vocabulary that simplifies DEI concepts, making them more accessible and actionable. This common language helps to break down barriers and misconceptions, ensuring that all team members are on the same page regarding DEI goals and objectives. By creating a unified understanding, the model facilitates more meaningful and productive conversations around diversity, equity, and inclusion. Leaders can better identify and address biases, advocate for equitable practices, and champion diversity initiatives. This leads to the development of inclusive leadership styles that are essential for driving organizational change. As leaders model inclusive behavior, they set the tone for the entire organization, encouraging others to follow suit.

The Ally to All-In model has become a powerful tool in my coaching toolbox that helps leaders access DEI conversations more effectively and creates a common language for driving inclusion. By fostering inclusive leadership and enhancing engagement, this framework not only supports individual growth but also drives organizational success, ensuring that DEI principles are deeply embedded in every aspect of the business. Organizations that embrace the Ally to All-In model see tangible benefits in terms of innovation, employee satisfaction, and overall performance.

The journey from Ally to All-In is ongoing, requiring continuous learning and commitment. Leaders navigating the framework often find themselves sliding back and forth between the steps because growth in DEI is not linear. This fluidity is essential, as each step—whether it's Awareness, Acknowledgment, Atonement, Accountability, or Amplification—offers ongoing opportunities for deeper learning, reflection, and action based on the unique challenges and contexts that arise. As a result, leaders may discover a new challenge that requires a second, third, or even fourth revisit of a previous step. When you are navigating your journey from Ally to All-In, it is important to first recognize and honor where you are in the process and ground yourself in that particular step, ensuring you approach each situation with the appropriate mindset and intention. The Ally to All-In model provides leaders with a structured pathway to deepen their understanding and involvement in DEI efforts over time. This sustained commitment ensures that DEI remains a core priority, driving lasting change and fostering a truly inclusive organizational culture.

Chapter 4

Awareness

OPENING OUR EYES: THE FIRST STEP TOWARD INCLUSION

"Awareness is the greatest agent for change."

ECKHART TOLLE

Awakening to Bias

Awareness. This is the most basic, yet profound tool in understanding the complexities of DEI. Growing up as a straight white male in a predominantly homogenous environment, I was largely unaware of the complexities and nuances of DEI. Yet, the first seeds of awareness were planted in my childhood, during a seemingly ordinary event that would leave a lasting impact on me.

I remember the day my parents put my childhood home on the market to sell. One evening, a neighbor stopped by, and I overheard a conversation that I didn't fully understand at the time. The neighbor expressed concern about my parents potentially "breaking up" the neighborhood. The phrase struck me as odd, and though I couldn't grasp the full meaning, I sensed the discomfort that came from the conversation, especially after the neighbor left and my parents huddled up in a conversation that they obviously did not want me to hear.

The next day, in my typical childhood pattern of asking incessant questions until I understood, I pressed my parents for answers. I wanted to know what the neighbor meant and why it had made them so uneasy. I remember feeling blown off a little bit as my parents tried to assure me that there was nothing for me to worry about. But their initial response just wasn't sitting well with me, so I kept coming back to my original question of what "breaking up" the neighborhood meant. I finally wore my mother down and she explained that the neighbor wanted to make sure that we sold our house to a white family. Though she did answer my question, I still did not understand what was driving so much concern. As a nine-year-old kid, race was not something that I thought about much. I went to school with a fairly diverse population of students and we all played together on the playground and on our sports teams. I never noticed there were only white families within my neighborhood, but it was suddenly something of which I was very aware. An awareness that expanded when we moved, and I realized that there was only one black family living in our new neighborhood.

This was my first glimpse of inequity. I noticed it. I questioned it. It bothered me, and then like any other short attention span child, I moved along to the next thing that piqued my interest. However, though I didn't have the language or the understanding to fully articulate it at the time, the experience planted a seed that would eventually grow into a deeper awareness of the inequities around me.

As I grew older and entered college, this awareness continued to evolve. In the diverse setting of my university, I encountered

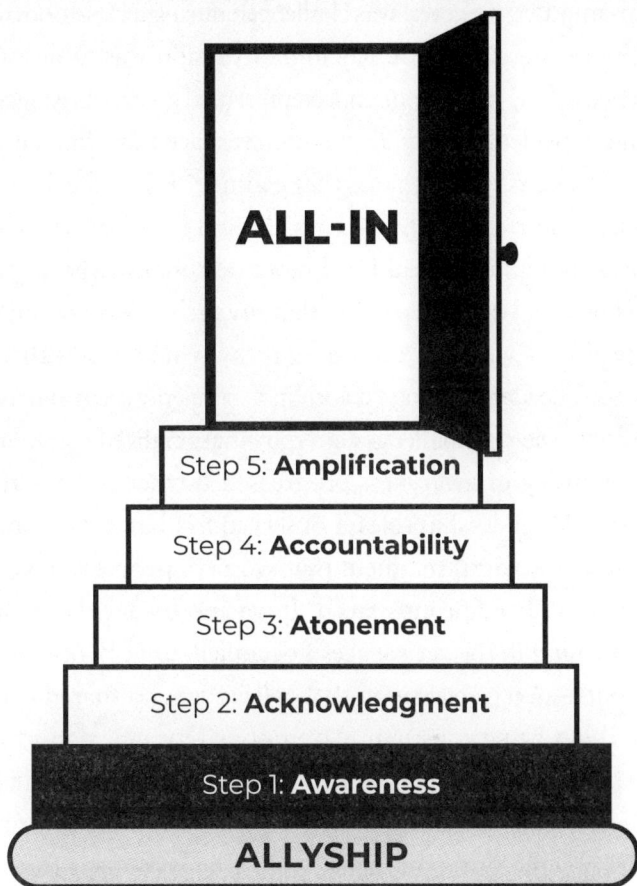

ALL-IN

Step 5: **Amplification**

Step 4: **Accountability**

Step 3: **Atonement**

Step 2: **Acknowledgment**

Step 1: **Awareness**

ALLYSHIP

perspectives and experiences far different from my own. However, during this time, I fell into the trap that many well-intentioned people do—I began to question why we needed to put people into boxes based on race, gender, or other identities. I thought the best path forward was to adopt a "colorblind" approach, believing that if we simply stopped calling out and harping on differences, the world would be a more equitable place.

This mindset, however, was challenged during a classroom discussion about systemic racism. My initial reaction was to dismiss the experiences of my peers from underrepresented groups as exaggerated or isolated incidents. After all, *I* had never faced discrimination, so how could it be as widespread as they claimed? But as the discussions continued, I started to listen—really listen. I heard stories of exclusion, bias, and injustice that I had never personally experienced but couldn't ignore. I began to realize that *my* reality was not universal; *my* experiences were not the standard by which others should be measured. The idea of being "colorblind" suddenly seemed naive and dismissive of the real challenges faced by marginalized communities.

My journey of awareness progressed further as I entered the workforce. In leadership roles, I observed firsthand the disparities in opportunities and treatment that women, people of color, and other marginalized groups faced. It was no longer theoretical; it was happening in the very spaces I occupied. One pivotal moment stands out—a conversation with a colleague who shared her frustration about being consistently overlooked for new opportunities despite her experience and qualifications. Her words struck a chord in me, and I realized that my silence and inaction were contributing to the problem. Systemic racism was a new concept for me, or maybe one that I conveniently ignored. As my awareness deepened, I came to realize that I was part of a system that upheld these inequities, even if unintentionally. For example, I remember sitting in a meeting where my colleague's ideas were ignored, and instead of calling attention to it, I stayed silent—choosing comfort over confrontation. By not speaking up, I was allowing the system that overlooked her to continue, effectively reinforcing the inequity I claimed to want to change.

My awareness around gender roles took on new urgency when I became a father to daughters. Thinking back on their childhood, my first glimpse of gender inequity occurred during their middle school years. Both of my daughters excelled in all of their classes throughout elementary school, but when they reached middle school, they were all of a sudden coming home saying that they weren't good at math and couldn't do it. This seemed strange to me, and I started to become aware of the conversations that were occurring around science, technology, engineering, and mathematics subjects and the tendency for female students to be steered away from them within the school system. I noticed how my daughters were often praised in subjects like English and art for their creativity and communication skills, but when it came to math or science, feedback was more critical or framed in ways that subtly discouraged their interest. I began to see the world through my daughters' eyes, imagining the challenges they might face simply because of their gender.

As they got older my daughters became my vehicles for greater awareness in a lot of ways. I remember them talking about a dance one year and they mentioned that two girls were taking one another as their dates. There wasn't any shock factor or judgment in their delivery. They were simply telling us who was taking whom to the dance, and one of the couples happened to be two girls. I also remember another dinner table conversation years later where they tried to explain the difference between the different types of sexual identities to my wife and me. Needless to say, it was educational and enlightening.

To be honest, as a white cisgender male, I was of two minds about it at the time. The less aware part of me thought, "No. I don't understand any of this. There are two genders and that's it." Conceptually, I had a hard time moving away from what I had been taught my whole life. On the other hand I thought, "Wow! How progressive. These kids feel so comfortable with these conversations that we were not even allowed to have when I was growing up." Of course, there were kids that we had assumed were gay, but they weren't allowed to be themselves and we were clearly not supposed to talk about it.

Once again, the glimpses of inequity were evolving my awareness. My daughters helped me realize that, from a personal and professional perspective, I needed to expand my awareness and put the things I was learning into practice, not just for them, but for all people who encounter barriers to equity in their personal and professional lives. These experiences over the years have forced me to confront my own privilege and biases. I had to accept that while I had worked hard to achieve my success, I had also benefited from a system that favored people like me, which was a hard truth to swallow, but it was a necessary one on my awareness journey.

Leadership Awareness: Eye-Opening Encounters

At the helm of a prestigious tech firm stood my client, James. He was a seasoned executive, known for his strategic acumen and unwavering determination. Yet, James found himself facing a challenge unlike any before—navigating the complex landscape of DEI. As a white male leader, James realized that embracing DEI couldn't just be a box to tick off in his leadership journey; it had to involve a fundamental shift in perspective and practice. With this realization James embarked on a quest to expand his awareness and understanding of the many nuances within the DEI conversation.

He understood that true awareness meant valuing the unique per-spectives and contributions of each individual within his organiza-tion. So, James did something bold—he decided to listen.

James set up meetings with employees from diverse back-grounds, creating a space where those who wanted to share their stories and experiences could do so voluntarily, ensuring they felt invited rather than obligated to educate him. From the quiet intern to the seasoned executive, he listened intently, absorbing the rich-ness of their insights. Through these conversations, James began to appreciate the depth of diversity within his organization—not solely in terms of race or gender but in perspectives, experiences, and talents.

With newfound awareness fueling his passion, James rallied his leadership team and reexamined the company's values and mission. They audited their recruitment processes, examining whether their job postings and job descriptions used inclusive language, and James worked closely with hiring managers to raise their awareness of unconscious bias in hiring decisions. In addition to recruitment, leadership took a close look at internal feedback systems to deter-mine whether adequate processes were in place to drive awareness around employee and workplace experiences.

As the firm evolved in its DEI mission, James came to see his awareness as the bedrock of true leadership. By analyzing every aspect of the organization with an eye to diversity, they were able to take the first steps toward the meaningful progress that would eventually transform their tech company into a beacon of inclusion and excellence.

Awareness is a multifaceted and critical aspect of leadership that starts with true self-reflection, a practice that often conflicts with the tenets of white male culture. White male leaders need to not only understand their strengths and skill sets, but also their weaknesses and motivations. Without this understanding, we continuously make uninformed decisions that can negatively impact our employees and organizations as a whole. Self-aware leaders recognize that their actions impact others, and they carry that knowledge with them when deciding whether to drive necessary change or close their eyes to uncomfortable realities.

Being aware and understanding our privilege is a critical first step, requiring a profound recognition of the systemic advantages that come with being white and male in society. For example, are you aware of how your privilege can show up as bias, whether conscious or unconscious? Unconscious biases can subtly influence decision-making processes, leading to disparities in hiring, promotion, and performance evaluation.

Think about James and his leadership of a tech company. In his awareness journey, he may notice a lack of diversity among his leadership team, a common issue within the tech field. Quite often, this stems from leaders recruiting and promoting in their own image. This is how our unconscious bias shows up. For instance, if James graduated from an Ivy League school, he may direct his recruitment team to look for candidates solely from Ivy League schools. Now, of course these universities have a vast talent pool of amazing STEM graduates, but let's at least acknowledge and become aware that there's also great students at other schools. Some of these students couldn't afford to go to an Ivy League school, but that doesn't mean they are not highly capable. When white male leaders recognize the ways that their privilege can inadvertently perpetuate disparities within the workplace, we can better advocate for equitable opportunities.

I led a virtual training session with a group of twelve leaders: two white women, one Asian man, and nine white men. Early on, I sensed one of the white men was clearly resistant to the ideas I was presenting. He kept questioning the need to categorize people, essentially advocating for a colorblind approach. He was vocal, arguing that labeling and categorizing people is more divisive than unifying.

To my surprise, Joe, the Asian man, unmuted himself and directly addressed his colleague. "When you claim to be color-blind," Joe said, "you're not only ignoring, but also diminishing, the unique experiences that shape who I am. These experiences are a source of pride for me, and I believe they bring value to this team." Others quickly chimed in, expressing their gratitude for Joe's perspective.

While I can't say for certain that the reluctant participant's views were permanently altered, there was a noticeable shift in his demeanor; and perhaps, his level of awareness. He became more open and receptive for the remainder of our session together. The conversation that ensued brought up an important point about the notion of "not seeing color" and how that can impact organizational leadership. It's an idea that a lot of white people are raised to believe. We are first taught to think this way by our parents, and then this idea gets reinforced throughout our lives, both as a defense against biased and racist acts we witness and, at times, those we ourselves commit. Now, I do recognize the assumption of equality that exists in this perspective, but there is also a great deal of naivete in failing to recognize the implicit advantage in the ability to even say, "I don't see color." Yes, it is a very aspirational way of thinking, but we are nowhere close to achieving that state. And when leaders try to lead through this lens, they lose an awareness of the systemic processes that already compartmentalize people based on their inclusion in historically disadvantaged groups. By ignoring people's experiences based on their race or gender we prevent ourselves from reaching a place of mutual appreciation and understanding that would allow us to ever achieve a "colorblind" society.

INCLUSIVE LEADERSHIP AT A GLANCE

Actively seek to broaden your perspective.

Inclusive leadership begins with awareness. As a leader, make a conscious effort to educate yourself about the diverse experiences and challenges faced by different groups. Attend workshops, read literature on diversity and inclusion, and engage in conversations with people from various backgrounds. By understanding the complexities of different identities and experiences, you can better recognize and address unconscious biases in your decision-making processes.

Corporate Awareness: Organizational Blindness

The racial justice events of 2020 were a wake-up call for organizational leaders around the world, even reaching the largest global corporations. For decades, executives had been patting themselves on the back about a bunch of activities that were not actually effective because the effects of systemic racism were so much deeper than most of us realized. I understand that might sound like a privileged statement because people from underrepresented communities have known this reality for a very long time, but for those of us who were proud of our ineffective diversity efforts, the awareness that exploded in the summer of 2020 was a game changer, shedding light on how much work remains undone. We had been sleepwalking our way through a bunch of these DEI efforts, and we needed to do a much better job of really thinking about how our systemic inequities were impacting not only our employees, but also the future of business. Through the empathy and perspective that can come from these realizations, leaders can deepen their understanding of the experiences of their diverse workforce.

From the outside looking in, the initial corporate awareness looked like a wave of public statements from a variety of corporate leaders, condemning racial injustice and expressing solidarity with the Black community. Tech company CEOs from Apple and Google offered personal statements to employees and customers declaring their commitment to equity and social justice. Nike used its vast platform to denounce racism and publicly support various racial justice organizations. This messaging, crafted to resonate with the emotion of the moment, demonstrated a growing awareness within the corporate world about the role that businesses play in upholding the systemic injustices of the world.

As I was living in the UK at the time, I learned about the 2020 racial justice movement in a couple of ways. The first was, like most of society, through the news reporting which was definitely presented through a British lens. There was an undercurrent of judgment that was coming through in some of the reporting—the US is out of control, it's barbaric, it's not safe. And seeing these clips on the television, I didn't recognize the US or the country that I called home based on these images. I found myself trying to interpret and explain away what was happening in the US to people I just happened to interact with on a daily basis. I remember getting into a taxi one time and when I spoke, the driver quickly picked up on my American accent and immediately began asking me all types of questions. What's happening in your country? Why are people so angry? What are the protests about? Interestingly, I also got asked questions about why it took so long for America to reach that point of frustration, which spoke to me as a criticism about our societal and individual lack of awareness. Sometimes I would engage, but other times, I just didn't have the energy for it. So, I'd say, "I'm Canadian," and look out the window—again, my privilege on full display.

But working for an American company at the time, I also witnessed a bit of a reckoning. I saw leaders analyzing our internal systems and asking the difficult questions. Based on my role, I was part of these conversations around awareness. Yes, there was some pushback, particularly from my UK peers who saw issues of inequity as exclusively belonging to the US. Thankfully, a couple of brave coworkers stood up to say, "Actually, we have a lot of the same issues here in the UK. They're just buried a little bit deeper in this country." In real time, I saw the beginnings of awareness within my organization, and how that initial spark can foster a sense of community and collaboration that drives organizational success.

Final Thought: The Cost of Ignorance

In today's climate, white male leaders cannot afford to willfully ignore the importance of awareness. From a business sense, we must plug into the diverse dynamics of our teams and the broader organizational culture. Otherwise, we maintain the status quo where team members feel unheard and alienated. We must also maintain a level of social awareness around our consumers and society in general. Today's consumer has high expectations for the brands that they support. They want to know what is being done both internally and externally to drive equity. Without the awareness needed to comprehend this current environment, white male leaders cannot adequately anticipate future challenges and adapt the strategies and approaches needed to meet changing circumstances. Socially aware leaders can create processes and plans that align with the long-term goals of the organization. They can also rally their team and position their organization to move forward in its diversity efforts.

Awareness is only the beginning of the All-In Framework. It wasn't enough for me to just recognize the problem; I had to do something about it. I began educating myself, seeking out perspectives different from my own, and engaging in difficult conversations. I learned that being an ally meant more than just standing on the sidelines—it required active participation and a willingness to challenge the status quo.

This journey has been both humbling and transformative. It has reshaped my view of DEI from a distant, abstract concept to a deeply personal and urgent responsibility. As a straight white man, I recognize that my voice carries weight, and I have a choice in how I use it. I can either contribute to the perpetuation of inequities, or I can be part of the solution. Today, I am committed to the latter. My journey of awareness has led me to a place of accountability and action. I strive to use my platform to amplify the voices of those who have been historically marginalized, to challenge systems of oppression, and to create inclusive environments where everyone can thrive.

Awareness is not a journey with a defined endpoint; it is ongoing, and I am continually learning. But I am no longer content with passive allyship. I am All-In, committed to being an active and engaged partner in the fight for equity and inclusion.

Tools for Building Awareness

Something You Can Do Right Now
Self-Reflection Exercise: Take a moment to reflect on your own biases and assumptions. Consider your upbringing, social circles, and life experiences, and how they may have shaped your perspectives and beliefs. Ask yourself questions such as: What biases might I hold, consciously or unconsciously? In what ways do my privileges influence my interactions and decision-making? Are there instances where I may have inadvertently contributed to exclusion or discrimination? Engaging in this self-reflection exercise can help you become more aware of your own biases and begin the journey toward mitigating their impact.

Something You Can Do This Week
Observation Challenge: Dedicate this week to observing and questioning workplace dynamics, with a focus on identifying potential areas for improvement in DEI. Pay attention to interactions between colleagues, patterns of communication, and decision-making processes. Look for signs of exclusion or bias, such as unequal opportunities for advancement, microaggressions, or lack of representation in leadership roles. Take notes on your observations and reflect on how these dynamics contribute to the overall workplace culture. This exercise can provide valuable insights into areas where your organization may need to prioritize DEI initiatives and interventions.

Something You Can Do This Month
DEI Training: Commit to participating in diversity training programs over the course of the month to deepen your understanding

and awareness of DEI issues. These training sessions may cover topics such as unconscious bias, privilege, systemic oppression, inclusive leadership, and creating equitable workplaces. Engage actively in the training sessions, asking questions, sharing insights, and reflecting on how the content applies to your role as a leader. Take the opportunity to learn from diverse perspectives and experiences. Consider how you can incorporate these learnings into your daily practices and decision-making processes. By investing in diversity training, you can enhance your knowledge and skills as a DEI advocate and contribute to creating a more inclusive workplace environment.

Chapter 5

Acknowledgment

FACING THE TRUTH: OWNING OUR ROLE IN THE SYSTEM

"You can't change what you don't acknowledge."

PHIL MCGRAW

Naming the Privilege

Acknowledgment. It's a word that sounds simple enough, but for me, it has become one of the most challenging yet powerful tools in my DEI journey—a journey that has been as much about uncovering truths within myself as it has been about engaging with the world around me.

I was raised in a society that subtly, and sometimes overtly, reinforced the idea that my experience as a white man was the "norm," the baseline against which everything else was measured. Like most white people, I was not raised to recognize whiteness as a racial identity, and this selective invisibility made it easy to avoid the acknowledgment of my own privilege. For a long time, I operated under the assumption that my hard work and determination were the sole drivers of my success. I believed in meritocracy and the idea that everyone started from the same point on the racetrack.

It was a comforting illusion that allowed me to exist within my own happy world. I did not have to confront the societal injustices that, in reality, provided me with a much higher chance of success based on my gender and race.

The first step in my journey toward acknowledgment came after I became aware that my experience moving through the world was not universal. The cracks in my worldview started to form through conversations with friends and colleagues, many of whom were women, people of color, or members of the LGBTQ+ community. They shared stories of obstacles they faced. Obstacles which I had never even considered, let alone encountered. These weren't just isolated incidents, they were patterns woven into the fabric of their daily lives. I began to see that the advantages I had taken for granted—the ease with which I could navigate professional spaces, the assumptions of competence that greeted me in every room—were not universally shared.

But acknowledgment isn't just about seeing what others experience; what moves awareness into acknowledgment is turning the lens inward. I had to confront the reality of my own identity as a white man and the ways in which that identity afforded me unearned advantages. This was not an easy process. It required me to let go of the idea that recognizing privilege meant diminishing my accomplishments. Instead, I came to understand that acknowledgment was about embracing a more complex, nuanced truth: that my success was both a product of my efforts and the societal structures that have historically favored people who look like me.

As I continued to reflect on this, I began to incorporate a new practice into my interactions. I started to explicitly acknowledge my identity in conversations by stating, "As a white man, here is

ALL-IN

Step 5: **Amplification**

Step 4: **Accountability**

Step 3: **Atonement**

Step 2: **Acknowledgment**

Step 1: **Awareness**

ALLYSHIP

how I approach the problem." While at times it felt a bit awkward, I found that this simple practice had a profound impact. It signaled to others that I was aware of my own identity and how it might influence the conversation. Moreover, it served as a constant self-reminder to be mindful and appreciative of all the identities and experiences present in the room. This wasn't just a personal exercise; I also encouraged my clients to adopt this practice. I found it created space for more honest, inclusive, and reflective dialogues, where everyone's perspectives were acknowledged and valued.

Acknowledging my own identity and privilege also meant accepting the discomfort that comes with it. It's one thing to intellectually understand privilege, it's another to sit with the unease that accompanies that realization. There were moments when I wanted to retreat back into the comfort of ignorance, to pretend that I didn't know what I now knew. But I realized that to do so would be a betrayal—not just of others, but of the person I was striving to become.

The next phase of acknowledgment was about putting voice to difficult situations and realities. In my professional life I had often shied away from conversations about race, gender, and inequality, fearing that I might say the wrong thing or unintentionally offend someone. But I came to understand that silence was not neutrality; it was complicity. Acknowledgment meant stepping into the discomfort of these conversations, even when it felt safer to remain silent. It meant being willing to make mistakes, to be corrected, and to learn in real-time.

One particular moment that stands out to me occurred early in my career. I was in a work meeting where I described one of my co-workers as a "slave driver." My intention was positive—I was impressed with how well she kept projects on track and held others accountable. One of the other participants in the meeting paused the flow of the conversation and pointed out that the term I used was racist, even though I had meant it as a compliment. The room went silent, as it often does when race is brought up. My instinct was to stay quiet, to let others jump into the conversation. But I knew that my acknowledgment of the situation—both of the issue at hand and of my own responsibility to acknowledge the term I used—was crucial.

Admittedly, my initial reaction was a mix of defensiveness and embarrassment. After all, it's a term that has been ingrained into our vernacular and I was far from being the only one in the office to use it. But on the other hand, how could I not have recognized the offensive history attached to it? I acknowledged my lack of awareness to the rest of the group in the meeting. It was a small act that opened my eyes to the power of acknowledgment. It underscored the importance of being aware of the language I use and how it impacts others. In acknowledging both my privilege and the difficult realities faced by others, I began to see how this practice could be transformative, not just for me, but for the spaces I inhabited. Acknowledgment became a bridge—a way to connect with others on a deeper level, to validate others' experiences, and to begin the process of change. It's not about having all the answers or being perfect; it's about showing up with honesty, humility, and a willingness to grow.

In the end, acknowledgment is not a destination but a practice— a daily commitment to seeing the world as it is, not just as I would like it to be. It's a practice that requires courage, vulnerability, and above all, a deep respect for the truth, no matter how uncomfortable it might be.

Courageous Conversations

Nestled within a towering office building, there was a prestigious law firm renowned for its long history of successful litigation and significant influence. Firm leaders prided themselves on the firm's formidable reputation and contributions to the legal field. Yet, beneath the polished exterior, the firm grappled with a legacy of exclusion and inequity that had been largely overlooked. David, a managing partner who had been with the firm for over twenty years, was also a new coaching client of mine. A white man in his mid-fifties, David saw himself as a fair and just leader, committed to the firm's success and his personal integrity. His career had been marked by numerous professional accomplishments, and he had always believed that his workplace was one based on equity. However, that perspective began to shift dramatically after he reluctantly attended a DEI seminar, which was mandated by the firm's HR team. Designed to challenge entrenched biases and shed light on systemic inequalities, the seminar delved deeply into the histories of systemic racism and the persistent barriers faced by marginalized communities. For David, the experience was eye-opening, forcing him to face some uncomfortable truths about the inequities that had pervaded his firm for decades.

Understandably, David's initial reaction was a mix of defensiveness and discomfort, but as the seminar progressed, these feelings gave way to a profound sense of responsibility. He realized that his prior notions of fairness had been limited and began to see the gaps in his understanding. He began to acknowledge that the firm's practices and culture had inadvertently perpetuated a cycle that disadvantaged individuals from diverse backgrounds.

That evening, David sat in his office, reflecting on the stories shared during the seminar. He recalled the words of a young Black attorney from his firm who spoke about feeling invisible and overlooked despite her hard work and dedication. This revelation struck a chord with David. He realized that, while he had always seen himself as an ally, he had never truly acknowledged the struggles faced by his colleagues of color. Determined to make a difference, he decided to make some changes in the way he showed up as a leader.

To begin this process, David implemented a strategy of acknowledging his own identity in DEI conversations. He began starting some of his remarks with phrases like, "Coming into this conversation as a white man . . ." It wasn't something he did in every meeting before every statement, but David found it to be an effective bridge for communication in situations where he experienced trouble getting through to a diverse audience or participating in conversations around DEI. He understood the value of acknowledgment in DEI as a tool for recognizing the existence of biases, privileges, and systemic structures that benefit some communities while creating barriers for others. The types of honest and open conversations that push DEI forward require safe spaces for individuals to share their experiences and perspectives. By acknowledging his identity and privilege, David effectively began to create that safe space as a leader.

Over the next year, the law firm underwent a significant cultural transformation as the once-silent voices of marginalized employees were finally heard. David's acknowledgment and subsequent actions set a powerful precedent. It demonstrated that leaders, especially those who have historically held power, could drive meaningful change by acknowledging identity and privilege and committing to a more equitable future. The firm's journey became a beacon of hope and a model for other organizations seeking to advance their DEI efforts.

Incorporating Acknowledgment into Leadership

Acknowledgment is a precursor to forward action, moving DEI from a theoretical concept to a practical, actionable initiative. For white male leaders in particular, acknowledging our privilege is a critical first step in understanding our roles within systems of power and oppression. It recognizes the unearned advantages we have benefited from based on race and gender; advantages that have often been taken for granted. But I also understand the uncertainties and fears that can hold us back from taking steps toward acknowledgment. It resonates back to white male culture and the expectation that we place on ourselves to always have the right answers. But when it comes to conversations around DEI, most of us are just learning which questions to ask, so we definitely don't have the answers. It's a realization that can strike a little bit of fear in us that we may be seen as unprepared or unknowledgeable, so we have a tendency to sit back and say nothing at all.

There is also past history that gets in the way. A history of white male leaders who have been chastised or faced retribution for saying the wrong thing. You make a statement seemingly in good faith and all of a sudden there's an employee relations complaint about you. I can relate to these fears and I understand why they cause leaders to retreat from DEI conversations. I would like to think that the vast majority of people don't walk around wanting to offend someone on purpose, so to face serious consequences for a misstep can feel overwhelming. But being All-In takes vulnerability, courage, and the willingness to step into the discomfort. It's about recognizing that our actions don't always match our intentions and being open to learning from those moments. This journey isn't about perfection; it's about consistently showing up, listening, and committing to do better.

When leaders understand that their success has not been solely due to hard work but also to societal structures that favor them, they can start to dismantle the myth of pure meritocracy that often prevails in corporate environments. I do believe in the power of meritocracy and the importance of rewarding talent and effort, but we must also acknowledge the significant role that gender, race, and social background play in shaping opportunities and outcomes. Only by recognizing these influences can we work toward creating a truly fair and equitable system.

The acknowledgment and understanding brings a sense of responsibility. White male leaders, once aware of their privilege, are empowered to take actionable steps toward promoting equity within their organizations. They recognize ways to use their positions of power in advocating for policies and practices that support diversity and inclusion. But acknowledgment is not just about admitting privilege, it is also about leveraging it to effect positive change. By embracing their role in perpetuating or dismantling systems of oppression, white male leaders can play a meaningful part in creating workplaces that value and uplift every individual.

When leaders openly acknowledge the existence of systemic barriers and biases, it validates the lived experiences of those who have been impacted by discrimination and exclusion. This validation creates a supportive environment where marginalized employees feel heard, valued, and empowered to participate in DEI conversations without fear of dismissal or gaslighting. Acknowledgment signals a significant cultural shift within the organization toward greater transparency and accountability.

Most white male leaders did not reach their level of achievement without being able to comfortably make declarations. Whether that looks like a speech behind a podium, leading a management meeting, or unapologetically stating our thoughts, we know how to acknowledge our own opinions with little fear or hesitation. Where we often fall short is acknowledging the thoughts and experiences of those around us. We also fail to recognize that many of our colleagues of color have fewer opportunities to speak in these situations, and when they do, their perspectives are often met with greater scrutiny or opposition. We rarely stop to attentively listen to the stories being shared by our employees and colleagues. And on the rare occasion that we do start to listen, we allow the discomfort of these conversations to either diminish the impact of what we have heard or we stop listening altogether. We accept the ignorance of not knowing because acknowledgment is disagreeable. And I understand why. It stirs up feelings of shame, guilt, and even helplessness, an emotional roller coaster that nobody wants to voluntarily ride. But once we do the work of acknowledging this discomfort and move toward recognizing that what we feel is only a small percentage of the intolerable circumstances experienced by historically disadvantaged communities, we can broaden our self-awareness and work toward true inclusivity.

Inclusive Leadership at a Glance

Acknowledge and validate the experiences of others.

Inclusive leaders create spaces where all voices are heard and valued. When team members share their experiences, especially those related to discrimination or exclusion, listen with empathy and without defensiveness. Acknowledge their feelings and the validity of their experiences. Additionally, recognize and acknowledge your own unearned advantages or privileges, which can influence your perspective and interactions. This acknowledgment is crucial in understanding the full scope of inclusion and in taking steps to address any biases that may arise.

Corporate Acknowledgment Setting the Example

For corporations, the acknowledgment of wrongdoings is crucial for restoring trust with consumers, the public, and stakeholders in general. When systemic inequities negatively impact historically disadvantaged communities, the transparency and honesty of a public acknowledgment can help rebuild reputation and reassure stakeholders that the company is committed to ethical practices. From a legal perspective, addressing wrongdoings can mitigate negative repercussions, potentially reducing the severity of penalties, fines, or legal actions. From the business perspective, by proactively acknowledging mistakes, corporations can demonstrate accountability and make a public commitment to furthering ethical practices, an approach that can protect the company's reputation and ensure more stable financial performance in the long term. Acknowledging wrongs also brings about internal improvements, leading to a healthier corporate culture. It signals to employees that the company values integrity and accountability, which can boost morale, loyalty, and productivity. Corporate acknowledgment is the key to long-term sustainability because forward movement requires recognition and learning from past wrongs.

In 2017, Uber faced significant scrutiny and backlash following a blog post by a former employee who made accusations about pervasive gender discrimination and harassment within the company.[1] The post described a toxic workplace culture ingrained with systemic bias and inadequate responses to harassment complaints. The statements ignited a broader public backlash and widespread criticisms about the company's culture from employees, customers, and the public. In response to the allegations, then-CEO of Uber Travis Kalanick issued a public apology acknowledging the seriousness of the issues raised and the shortcomings in the corporation's handling of gender discrimination. He expressed regret for the company's failure to address these problems effectively and committed to making significant changes.

In 2021, Adobe made a public acknowledgment around the pervasive gender pay gap that continues to exist between the earnings of men and women, a pervasive issue of inequality within the workforce, but one that corporations have been slow to acknowledge.[2] Adobe apologized after an internal report revealed that gender pay disparities existed despite the company's previous assurances of pay equity.

Nationally, white men, on average, earn more compared to women of various racial and ethnic backgrounds. Look at the numbers:

- White women earn approximately 80-85 cents for every dollar earned by white men, reflecting a significant gender pay gap within the same racial group.[3]
- Black women face a wider gender pay gap, earning about 63-68 cents for every dollar earned by white men, demonstrating a combination of racial and gender discrimination.[4]
- Hispanic or Latina women experience one of the most pronounced pay gaps, earning approximately 55-60 cents for every dollar earned by white men.[5]
- Asian women generally earn more than Black and Hispanic women but still less than white men. On average, they make about 75-80 cents for every dollar earned by white men though it's important to note that the

Asian demographic is diverse, and earnings can vary significantly among different Asian subgroups.[6]
- Native American women also face a significant gender pay gap, earning approximately 60-65 cents for every dollar earned by white men.[7]

As these figures illustrate, the gender pay gap is compounded by race and ethnicity. While all women generally earn less than white men, women of color experience deeper disparities due to the intersection of both racial and gender biases. In 2019, Google apologized for gender pay disparities also uncovered in its internal pay equity analysis.[8] The company acknowledged that women at Google were paid less than their male counterparts for similar roles and pledged to address the disparities by adjusting salaries, increasing transparency, and enhancing its practices related to compensation and performance evaluations.

Numerous companies followed suit in 2020, apologizing for historical gender bias in hiring, compensation, and promotion practices. These public statements demonstrated the willingness of many corporations to acknowledge a prominent DEI problem. In recent years, we have also seen a growing number of companies acknowledge their biased actions and stances in relation to LGBTQ+ equity.

In 2017, the chief marketing officer of global lingerie company Victoria's Secret made statements supporting the exclusion of transgender and plus sized models in the company's marketing campaigns.[9] The following day, he apologized for his remarks, resigning from his position shortly thereafter. In 2020, Victoria's Secret publicly apologized for its systemic lack of inclusion, specifically mentioning the absence of transgender and plus-sized models in its branding.[10]

The racial reckoning of 2020 gave us countless examples of corporate acknowledgment, with one of the most infamous being the Black Square Movement where numerous companies used their social media platforms to acknowledge systemic racial injustice. Major brands like Walmart, Netflix, Adidas, and Amazon joined celebrities, influencers, and ordinary social media users in pausing regular content and encouraging people to educate themselves about systemic racism. Intended as a moment of solidarity and awareness-raising, this symbolic acknowledgment ignited a trend of corporations publicly acknowledging both systemic and societal wrongs. While this type of recognition is important, it is only the beginning of the All-In journey because without action, acknowledgment can quickly be interpreted as performative, which became the eventual criticism of the Black Square Movement.

Final Thought: The Power of Owning Our Stories

Acknowledgment sets a powerful example for others to follow. When white male leaders openly acknowledge their privilege and engage in DEI conversations, it sends a clear message to their teams and the broader organization. By leading by example, leaders inspire others to confront biases, challenge discrimination, and actively participate in creating a more inclusive workplace culture. This ripple effect can catalyze broader cultural change and drive meaningful progress toward diversity, equity, and inclusion. The journey is not easy, but it is essential for creating a future where everyone has the opportunity to thrive.

Tools for Practicing Acknowledgment

Something You Can Do Right Now
Self-Acknowledgment Exercise: Take a moment to engage in a self-acknowledgment exercise. Reflect on your own privileges, experiences, and potential biases. Consider aspects of your identity where you hold privilege, such as race, gender, sexual orientation, or socioeconomic status. Write down a list of these aspects and contemplate how they may impact your interactions with others in the workplace. Reflect on past experiences where your privilege may have influenced your perceptions or actions. By acknowledging your own privilege and biases, you can begin to cultivate greater self-awareness and empathy toward others.

Something You Can Do This Week
Listening Sessions: Schedule one-on-one listening sessions with team members from diverse backgrounds. Actively listen to their experiences and challenges, creating a safe space for them to share openly. Acknowledge the validity of their perspectives and avoid judgment or defensiveness. Instead, focus on understanding their unique points of view and empathizing with their experiences. Ask open-ended questions to encourage them to share their stories and insights. By engaging in these listening sessions, you demonstrate your commitment to understanding and supporting your team members, fostering trust and inclusivity within the workplace.

Something You Can Do This Month
Organizational Acknowledgment Workshop: Collaborate with HR or DEI specialists to create an organizational acknowledgment

workshop. Bring together employees from across the organization to discuss the importance of acknowledgment in creating a more inclusive workplace culture. Share success stories of acknowledgment initiatives and discuss their positive impact on employee morale, engagement, and retention. Facilitate open dialogue and encourage participants to share their personal experiences related to acknowledgment, both positive and challenging. By hosting this workshop, you create a forum for meaningful conversation and learning, empowering employees to acknowledge their own biases and privileges and work toward building a more equitable workplace for all.

Chapter 6

Atonement

MAKING AMENDS: TAKING RESPONSIBILITY FOR PAST HARMS

"True atonement isn't just saying 'I'm sorry;'
it's making things right and learning from the past
to build a better future."

UNKNOWN

Making Amends

Atonement. It's a word that carries weight, often associated with deep introspection and the need to make amends. In my journey through DEI as a white man, atonement has become a crucial step—a necessary act of reckoning with the mistakes I've made and the harm I may have caused, even unintentionally.

A pivotal moment that brought the power of atonement into sharp focus for me occurred in my role as the accountable executive for our organization's diversity efforts while based in the UK. The diversity team, the majority of whom were women, approached me with a concern. They highlighted that a leadership gender equity charter, which we had publicly agreed to, was up for renewal. My reaction was swift—I expressed that I did not want to re-up the charter. The honest answer was that it had created all sorts of headaches with reporting and falling short of expectations. It was my responsibility to provide a status report to the board on a quarterly basis and although we were making progress, we were not having the level of success that we aimed to have. The accountability for that fell onto my shoulders and I absolutely hated having to constantly explain it to the board. A lot of inconvenience and discomfort existed around it for me and my reputation, so in my opinion, the easiest path forward was to simply let the charter lapse, a stance that I suspected the board would support.

During that conversation with the team, they did push back a bit. They were clearly frustrated and annoyed with me, but it was ultimately my decision and I made it clear that my decision to let the charter lapse was final. I am generally a decisive leader, but I did walk away with a nagging feeling that I may have been missing something.

The next day, the team initiated the conversation again, something that they rarely did in response to my decisions. They told me that they found my decision short-sighted and that they felt I was letting my own identity as a male cloud my judgment. It felt like a harsh conversation starter, but it definitely piqued my attention. We sat down and had another discussion about how important it was for them, as women, to have representation in the leadership ranks. They again shared a compelling case that made me question what was really driving my decision. I began to realize that I had prioritized my own convenience and reputation over the greater importance of this DEI initiative. It reminded me that I bring my own biases and identity into my decision-making process, whether I'm aware of that or not.

We ultimately decided to renew the charter despite the inconvenience it might create. But acknowledging my mistake was only

ALL-IN

Step 5: **Amplification**

Step 4: **Accountability**

Step 3: **Atonement**

Step 2: **Acknowledgment**

Step 1: **Awareness**

ALLYSHIP

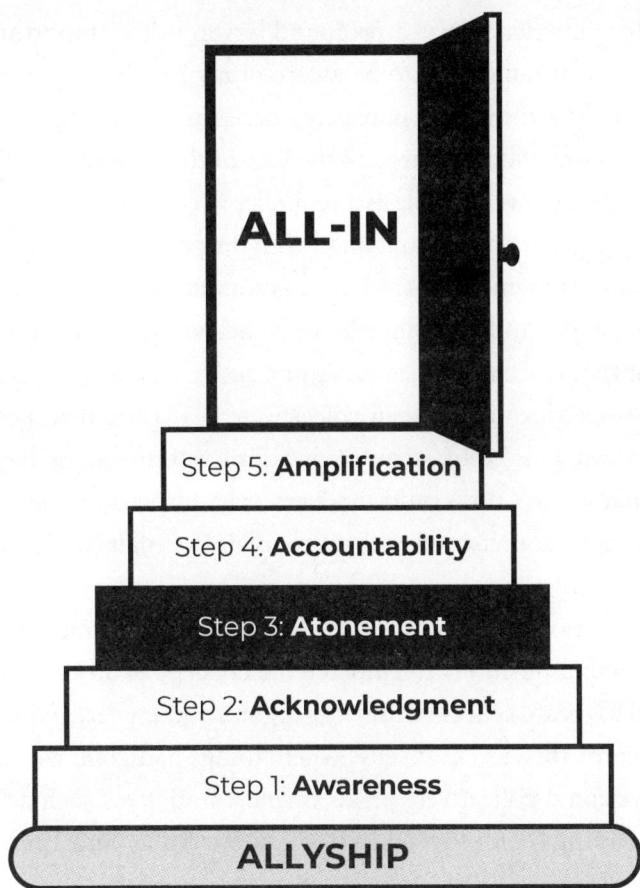

the first step toward atoning for my actions. I knew I had to go further. I sought out my team to apologize, not just for the specific incident, but for the broader impact of my actions. I wanted to convey that I understood the gravity of the lack of gender representation and that I was committed to making things right. This wasn't just about saying "sorry;" it was about taking responsibility and demonstrating my commitment to doing better.

This experience was a profound lesson in the importance of atonement. It taught me to be aware of my privilege and identity and how these things can impact my decision-making and it taught me to filter my actions through the lens of this knowledge. I often think back on this example as a reminder to continuously check my biases and ensure my actions align with the principles of equity and inclusion. Atonement, I learned, is not a one-time act. It requires ongoing effort and a willingness to be held accountable. I made it a point to involve my colleagues more actively in decision-making processes, ensuring that their voices were heard and their perspectives valued. I also took steps to educate myself further on the ways in which my actions could inadvertently perpetuate inequality, seeking out resources and engaging in dialogues that challenged my understanding.

In addition to my personal efforts, I began encouraging others in leadership positions to embrace the concept of atonement. We started to create spaces within our organization where individuals could come forward to discuss where things had gone wrong and how we could collectively make amends. Initiatives such as town hall meetings, employee advisory committees and Employee Resource Groups (ERGs) are excellent strategies. In today's interconnected world, companies can't just operate in a bubble. They need to engage in open dialogues with a wide range of stakeholders and listen to their concerns. It's not about assigning blame, but about fostering a culture of growth. As leaders, we must recognize that mistakes happen, but it is our responses to those mistakes and willingness to atone for them that define our commitment to DEI.

Atonement also required me to let go of the need to be seen as "good" or "right" all the time. It meant accepting that I would make mistakes, and that these mistakes could cause harm, regardless of my intentions. This was perhaps the hardest lesson to learn—understanding that my actions, even when well-meaning, could contribute to the very systems of oppression I sought to dismantle. But it was also the most liberating, because it allowed me to approach my work with greater humility and openness to growth.

When people hear the word "atonement," the idea of reparations often comes to mind. But that's not what this is about. Atonement, in the context of my DEI journey, is not about financial compensation or material restitution. Rather, it's about acknowledging the harm caused by my actions—whether intentional or not—and taking steps to repair relationships and rebuild trust. It's about the personal work of making amends, which lays the groundwork for stronger relationships that serve as a living demonstration of the power of working together to overcome past mistakes and build a more equitable future.

Turning Apology into Action

Michael, a manufacturing company CEO, had been with his company for over twenty years. A white man in his forties, Michael had always considered himself an inclusive leader. However, it wasn't until he received feedback via an all-employee sentiment survey that he began to see the gaps in his understanding. The survey, which delved deep into engagement and inclusion, revealed a high level of dissatisfaction among employees from historically underrepresented populations regarding a lack of inclusion and representation at the leadership levels. He partnered with me to dig deeper into the findings. The results of the survey revealed that there would likely be a high level of attrition in the next year, which would unwind many of the efforts that had been made to recruit diverse talent into the organization. Michael was forced to confront the uncomfortable truth about the inequities that were pervasive within his company leadership for decades.

Atonement is a critical yet underleveraged practice for leaders, particularly for white male leaders. At its core, atonement signifies a deep acknowledgment and understanding of past wrongs, both personal and systemic, and the commitment to rectify these injustices. For leaders in positions of power, this process is not merely a symbolic gesture but a foundational step toward fostering genuine inclusivity and equity within their organizations.

Atonement requires an honest reckoning with the historical and ongoing disparities that have marginalized various groups. For white male leaders, this means recognizing how systemic racism, sexism, and other forms of discrimination have shaped and continue to shape societal structures and workplace dynamics. This acknowledgment is essential because it confronts the privileges that have been unearned and often unnoticed. While some may argue that these issues are rooted in a distant past—something our ancestors did and are therefore irrelevant today—it's crucial to understand that the impact of these injustices persists in the present. The disparities we see in opportunities, representation, and treatment are a direct legacy of these historical inequities, continuously affecting marginalized communities. By acknowledging this, leaders can better understand the experiences and challenges faced by these groups, and actively work to dismantle these enduring barriers.

Determined to make a change, Michael called a meeting with the company's leadership team and then scheduled an all-hands meeting. He openly addressed the company's historical biases and the systemic barriers that had hindered the advancement of under-represented employees. This admission was met with a mixture of surprise and relief. Many employees had been waiting for this level of openness for years, and Michael's honesty laid the groundwork for rebuilding trust.

Recognizing that acknowledgment was only the first step, Michael initiated a series of concrete actions to address these disparities. The company offered DEI training for all managers, revised its recruitment and promotion processes to ensure equity, and established a mentorship program aimed at supporting engineers from underrepresented backgrounds.

Over the next year, the company underwent a significant cultural transformation. The voices of marginalized employees, once overlooked, were now beginning to be heard and acknowledged in meaningful ways. The mentorship program thrived, with senior engineers actively supporting and guiding their junior colleagues. The company's leadership team became more diverse, reflecting a broader range of perspectives and experiences.

Michael's actions exemplify a key aspect of atonement, which is a personal and public commitment to change. It is not enough to simply recognize past and present inequities; leaders must actively engage in efforts to dismantle the structures that perpetuate them. This commitment can manifest in numerous ways, including the implementation of policies that promote diversity, fostering an inclusive culture, and holding oneself and others accountable for actions that uphold or undermine DEI principles. This active engagement signals to all members of the organization that the leader is dedicated to creating a more equitable environment, thereby fostering a sense of belonging among marginalized groups and building a company culture based in trust.

Atonement is a powerful model of humility and sets the groundwork for accountability. When white male leaders openly acknowledge their own complicity in systemic injustices and demonstrate a willingness to learn and grow, they set a precedent for others to follow. This modeling can inspire a broader cultural shift within the organization, encouraging all employees to reflect on their own biases and behaviors and to take meaningful steps toward change. It also highlights that leadership is not about infallibility but about the courage to admit mistakes and the resolve to make amends.

Michael's admission and subsequent actions set a powerful precedent. He publicly admitted that, under his leadership, certain voices had been overlooked and opportunities for diverse employees had been stifled due to outdated policies and unconscious biases in hiring and promotions. To address this, Michael personally championed DEI initiatives in leadership meetings. His actions demonstrated that leaders, especially those who hold power, could drive meaningful change by owning past missteps and actively working toward a more equitable future. His example was one that his leadership team followed to make amends and build trust deeper within the organization. The company's journey became an example of progress and a model for other organizations seeking to advance their inclusion efforts.

Michael's story illustrates the transformative power of atonement. Before his journey, Michael's leadership perpetuated an environment where diverse voices were often overlooked, and opportunities were unevenly distributed due to unconscious biases and outdated practices. Recognizing this, he confronted these inequities head-on by openly acknowledging his role in the problem and implementing tangible changes, such as equitable hiring processes and mentorship programs for underrepresented employees. As a result, the culture of his organization began to shift—trust grew, inclusivity deepened, and employees felt empowered to bring their full selves to work. This journey was not easy, but it demonstrates that by taking accountability and committing to concrete actions, leaders can create an environment where everyone has the opportunity to thrive.

Atoning for Leadership Gaps

In my coaching practice, I have noticed that for many leaders, particularly white male leaders, fully embracing atonement in their leadership journey can be challenging. Atonement involves acknowledging past mistakes, taking responsibility for one's actions, and making amends, which can be a deeply personal and sometimes uncomfortable process. Several factors contribute to this hesitation. Firstly, the fear of blame and shame can be a significant barrier, as admitting to past mistakes tied to systemic issues like racism or sexism can evoke feelings of guilt and damage to reputation. Additionally, recognizing and addressing personal biases and privileges can feel threatening to one's established position of power and influence, creating resistance to the idea of atonement. Some leaders may not fully understand the importance of atonement in the DEI journey, seeing it as unnecessary or performative. The discomfort with vulnerability, perceived as a weakness, also deters leaders from openly admitting to mistakes and demonstrating a willingness to learn and grow. Lastly, the fear of legal and professional repercussions from admitting to past discriminatory practices can prioritize self-protection over genuine efforts to address and rectify past wrongs.

To overcome these hesitations, it is crucial to create a supportive environment where leaders feel safe to acknowledge their mistakes and take responsibility. Education on the importance of atonement in the DEI journey, coupled with concrete examples of positive outcomes from leaders who have embraced this process, can help mitigate fears and foster a culture of accountability and growth. Encouraging open dialogue, providing resources for personal development, and emphasizing the long-term benefits of atonement for both individuals and organizations are key steps in helping leaders fully embrace this critical aspect of their DEI journey.

INCLUSIVE LEADERSHIP AT A GLANCE

Take responsibility and make amends for past mistakes.

No leader is perfect, and acknowledging past missteps is crucial. If you or your organization have made errors or overlooked issues that affected inclusivity, own up to them. Apologize sincerely and outline concrete steps you will take to address and rectify the situation. Atonement isn't just about saying sorry; it's about demonstrating a genuine commitment to change and improvement.

Organizational Atonement

As discussed in the previous chapters, the 2020 protests brought about a wave of corporations publicly announcing their newly found awareness and many went on to acknowledge the roles that their industries and internal practices have played in maintaining societal and workplace disparities. But as we move through the framework from statements into action, the number of companies and organizations committing to atoning for past wrongs significantly decreases. Dismantling decades of inequality is a heavy task, but for companies that make atonement efforts, the payoff can be instrumental in growing the business and fostering both employee and consumer loyalty.

Prior to its surprising and controversial reversal in 2025, retail chain Target had taken numerous steps toward atonement through financial investments, community engagement, and internal DEI efforts. In an effort to drive economic growth and support for Black entrepreneurs, the company pledged to spend $2 billion with Black-owned businesses by the end of 2025.[1] Target significantly increased the number of products from Black-owned brands available in its stores and online, a step that established the company as a go-to retailer for diversified product offerings. This investment also provided Black-owned companies with financial investments, valuable retail mentorship, and networking opportunities.

Internally, Target leadership launched initiatives to ensure fair and equitable hiring practices with goals to increase representation of diverse team members at all levels, including key leadership roles. They cultivated an inclusive environment through the implementation of policies that protect and affirm LGBTQ+ employees, including strict anti-discrimination measures, inclusive health benefits, and support for transitioning employees.

Target atoned for its lack of inclusion among its supply chain by actively seeking and engaging with diverse suppliers across various categories, ensuring that these businesses are integrated into the community's procurement processes. This atonement extended to the retailer's marketing and advertising practices, which were consistently representative of diverse identities that portrayed a broad spectrum of experiences and stories. These steps highlighted Target's commitment to addressing historical and systemic inequities for both their employees and customers. My hope is that Target will reaffirm its commitment to this work, as it has previously been a standout in this space.

Many other major corporations took similar steps in response to the racial reckoning of 2020. Procter & Gamble (P&G) committed $5 million to support organizations fighting for racial equality and pledged additional funds to drive economic empowerment within the Black community.[2] The company also produced award-winning films designed to spark conversations about the everyday challenges faced by Black Americans and launched "Widen the Screen," an initiative aimed at expanding the representation of Black life in advertising and media.

The banking industry has provided numerous examples of atonement since 2020, actions that are long overdue. Systemic racism and discriminatory practices have been rooted within American financial infrastructure since its beginning, pushing the wealth gap that persists between white households and households of color. In the early twentieth century, discriminatory practices were legally and socially enforced, including the notorious practice of redlining, where banks denied access to financial services in certain communities based on their racial composition. The Home Owners' Loan Corporation, a government program established under The New Deal, created maps that marked predominantly Black neighborhoods in red, indicating them as high-risk areas for mortgage lending.[3] This practice persisted for decades, systematically denying Black and Brown families access to homeownership, a primary means of wealth-building in America.

While the Fair Housing Act of 1968 aimed to eliminate discrimination in housing and mortgage lending, discriminatory practices persisted.[4] Enforcement of federal laws and compliance have been inconsistent, and in the late 20th and early 21st centuries, we saw these systematic practices take on more subtle forms. For instance, the housing boom of the early 2000s was driven by the targeting of subprime loans to Black and Latinx borrowers. With highly unfavorable lending terms, such as higher interest rates and fees, these predatory loans left many of these homeowners in foreclosure and even more burdened with debt.

The banking industry faced an unprecedented backlash in 2020 with pressure from regulators, advocacy groups, and the public to improve equitable access to financial services. In response, several institutions have launched programs to increase lending to minority-owned businesses, invest in underserved communities, and improve diversity within their organizations. JPMorgan Chase pledged $30 billion over five years with a focus on advancing racial equity in homeownership through affordable housing and providing small business support in Black and Latinx communities.[5] Wells Fargo's Open for Business Fund allocated $400 million to support small businesses, particularly those owned by people of color.[6] The bank also undertook a comprehensive overhaul of its corporate culture, and set ambitious diversity and inclusion goals, including increasing the representation of underrepresented groups in its workforce and leadership.

Atonement efforts within the financial sector have also included advocacy efforts to support policies that address racial disparities in the broader financial system, including a push for reforms in lending practices and financial education programs. Through initiatives such as expanding access to banking services in under-served communities and promoting the use of alternative credit scoring methods, the banking industry can address the deep systemic inequities that affect communities of color. Significant challenges remain, but consistent efforts at atonement can keep us moving toward a more equitable banking system.

Major League Baseball (MLB) offered one of the best examples of atonement that I have witnessed. Between 1920 and 1948, the Negro Baseball Leagues provided a vital opportunity for African-American and Latino players to showcase their talent in a professional setting, offering a venue to play and compete at a high level after being barred from the major leagues due to racial segregation.[7] In 2020, the MLB officially recognized the teams in the Negro Leagues as major league teams, acknowledging the immense contributions of its players who had been excluded from MLB.[8] Then, in 2024, the MLB took an additional step toward atonement by not just celebrating the individual achievements of Negro League players, but also updating its record books to include their statistics, acknowledging that, despite playing under inferior conditions and lower pay, these talented players were among the best to have ever played the game.[9] This is the type of action that corrects historical injustices.

Final Thought: Taking Action Beyond Apologies

Atonement can bridge gaps and build stronger, more authentic relationships. When leaders genuinely atone, they create space for honest dialogue and mutual understanding. This process helps to heal wounds and build trust, which are essential for any collaborative effort toward DEI goals. It also empowers those who have been marginalized to share their stories and perspectives, enriching the organizational culture with diverse viewpoints and fostering innovation and creativity.

Atonement also offers a level of personal accountability that leads to growth and self-improvement. The process of atonement requires an understanding of the pain inflicted on others by discriminatory processes and systems. It involves a sense of empathy and compassion for others, which are key components of positive interpersonal relationships. As white males, atonement allows us to confront our own complicity by recognizing our privilege and taking responsibility for our inaction. It encourages self-reflection and introspection, which is a major step on the road to our emotional healing. Atonement helps us to replace those feelings of guilt and shame with the sense of responsibility and empowerment that feels familiar. By taking action, we can alleviate our negative emotions by addressing the root causes.

Atonement gives us the sense of responsibility that is crucial for our personal and professional development, leading us to make more mindful and conscientious decisions in the future. Through atonement, leaders can build trust, inspire others, and foster an organizational culture that values and promotes diversity, equity, and inclusion. This transformative process not only benefits the individuals within the organization but also strengthens the organization as a whole, making it more resilient, innovative, and just.

Ultimately, atonement is a bridge to accountability, the next critical step in my DEI journey. Atonement is about recognizing the harm and beginning the process of repair, but accountability ensures that the lessons learned lead to lasting change. It's about creating structures and practices that prevent future harm and holding myself and others responsible for upholding the values we aspire to.

Through atonement, I've learned to take ownership of my mistakes and ensure they are not repeated. I realized that acknowledgment alone was not enough. While recognizing my privilege and the impact of my actions was important, I started to understand that without taking steps to actively make amends, the impact of my journey would remain insular. Atonement begins the process of involving others on your DEI journey.

As leaders, especially white men, we must embrace atonement as an important step toward genuine and active participation in the DEI conversation. Only then can we create a world where equity is not just an ideal, but a reality.

Tools for Effective Atonement

Something You Can Do Right Now

Apology Letters: Take immediate steps to address any past actions or decisions that may have inadvertently contributed to inequality. Reflect on instances where your behavior, choices, or policies may have had a negative impact on individuals or groups within your organization or community. Write personalized apology letters to those affected, acknowledging the specific harm caused and expressing sincere regret. In your letters, clearly state your commitment to positive change and outline steps you are taking to prevent similar issues in the future. This act of atonement demonstrates accountability and a genuine desire to make amends, fostering a culture of trust and respect.

Something You Can Do This Week

Educational Webinar on Historical Injustices: Organize or participate in an educational webinar that focuses on historical injustices relevant to your industry or community. Invite experts or historians to share their insights on how past wrongs have shaped present disparities. Encourage open discussion among participants, allowing them to explore the lasting implications of these injustices and consider how they continue to affect marginalized groups today. By facilitating this learning opportunity, you help raise awareness, promote understanding, and inspire collective responsibility for addressing and rectifying historical inequities.

Something You Can Do This Month

Implement Corrective Actions: Collaborate with HR and organizational leadership to identify areas where historical discrimination or biases may have occurred within your organization. Conduct a thorough review of policies, practices, and workplace culture to uncover any lingering effects of past injustices. Develop and implement corrective actions or new policies designed to rectify these wrongs and prevent their recurrence. This may include revising hiring practices, offering training programs, providing resources for affected employees, and establishing accountability measures. By taking concrete steps to address and rectify historical discrimination, you demonstrate a strong commitment to creating a more equitable and inclusive environment for all employees.

Chapter 7

Accountability

WALKING THE WALK: HOLDING OURSELVES TO HIGHER STANDARDS

"Accountability is the glue that ties commitment to the result."

BOB PROCTOR

Learning To Be Held Accountable

Accountability. It's a word that carries both responsibility and action. In my DEI journey as a white man, accountability has become an essential cornerstone, moving beyond mere awareness, acknowledgment, and atonement to actively creating change and committing to continuously upholding the changes I have implemented.

Early on in my DEI work, I often thought that awareness and acknowledgment were enough. I believed that by recognizing my privilege and learning from my mistakes, I was doing my part. That made me a good ally, right? But over time, I realized that I required much more. It wasn't just about seeing or admitting where things had gone wrong. It was about being responsible for making sure those things didn't happen again and holding both myself and others to a higher standard.

On a personal level, raising two Gen Z daughters has built a natural level of accountability into my life. Their generation has an expectation of inclusivity and equity that is almost instinctual. My daughters are not afraid to call me out when I fall short of that standard. Whether it's language I've used or a viewpoint I've expressed, they hold me accountable in ways that are sometimes uncomfortable, but always necessary. I've come to see their feedback as not only an opportunity for growth, but a form of accountability that constantly reminds me that DEI isn't just something that happens at work—to truly be All-In, it's a value I must live out in every aspect of my life.

In the workplace, one specific example stands out where accountability was crucial. My team and I were responsible for updating the restroom facilities in our building, and as part of the upgrade, we decided to include gender-neutral restrooms. Initially, it seemed like a straightforward decision that aligned with our inclusivity goals. However, due to building codes, plumbing requirements, and unforeseen complexities, the implementation became more complicated than we anticipated.

In one high-traffic area of the building, the most practical solution was to convert a designated disabled restroom into a gender-neutral restroom. Without consulting anyone, the builder created a sign indicating that the restroom was now designated as both a disabled and gender-neutral space. It didn't take long for employees to notice and communicate their complaints. Disabled employees voiced concerns of feeling displaced and deprioritized, while nonbinary employees took issue with the suggestion that they were somehow linked to being labeled "disabled." These were unintentional messages, but hurtful nonetheless. Even though the

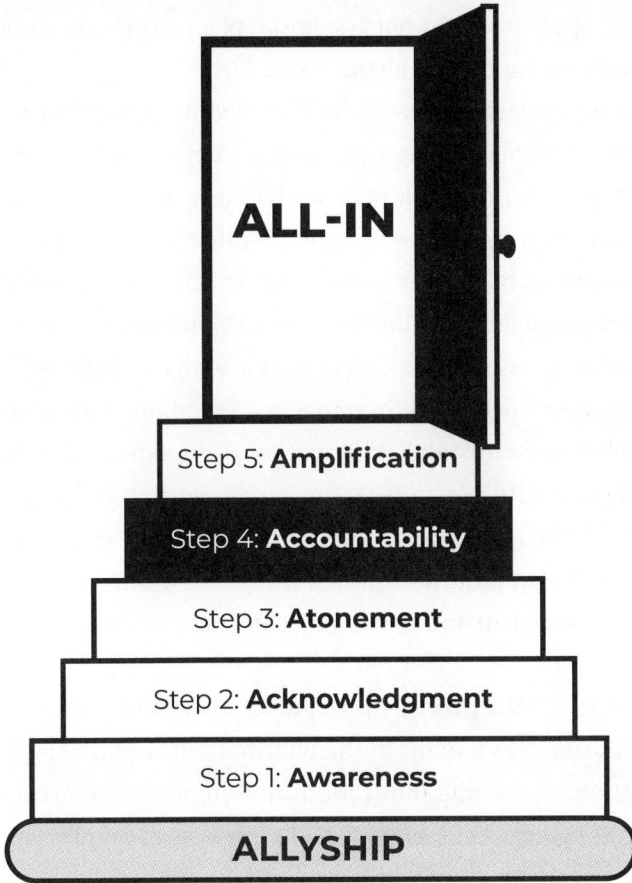

ALL-IN

Step 5: **Amplification**

Step 4: **Accountability**

Step 3: **Atonement**

Step 2: **Acknowledgment**

Step 1: **Awareness**

ALLYSHIP

team's intention was positive, the communication and execution were poorly handled. Given that I was responsible for the facilities as part of my role, I was accountable for that decision, and it was clear that we had missed the mark. I had to own up to the fact that we didn't think through the implications properly, nor did we consult with those who these decisions would most affect. It was a humbling moment, but accountability demanded that I fix the problem, apologize, and put systems in place to prevent something like this from happening again.

We immediately fixed the bathroom signage to make it all-inclusive. We also set up a committee so that as we were thinking about future building changes we had a forum where we could request and leverage employee input. In reality, not all feedback could be implemented, but at least we were able to acknowledge the requests and provide an explanation for our actions. We created an open dialogue as opposed to making decisions with no employee input.

The experience taught me that accountability isn't just about acknowledging a mistake; it's about correcting these mistakes and ensuring that future actions are more thoughtful and inclusive. It reinforced the idea that accountability requires more than just intention. It also requires follow-through—both in correcting the immediate problem and in creating safeguards for the future.

Stepping Up to Accountability

Apex Pharma was a giant in the pharmaceutical industry, known for its groundbreaking innovations and impressive market share. Despite its success, the company had a less visible, yet pressing issue: a lack of diversity and inclusivity within its ranks. At the helm of the HR organization was John, a white male who had been with the company since its early days.

Through our coaching sessions I learned that John had always considered himself a progressive HR leader. However, as societal conversations around DEI became more prominent, he realized that both he and his company were falling short. Employees of color, women, and other underrepresented groups often felt marginalized and excluded from key opportunities. John knew that acknowledging these issues was not enough. He needed to hold himself and his organization accountable to drive real change.

Firstly, accountability requires leaders to recognize the influence of their actions and decisions on their organization's culture and on the individuals within it. For white male leaders, this means understanding how their positions of power and privilege have historically shaped, and continue to shape, the experiences of their employees. By acknowledging this influence, leaders can begin to see where systemic inequities exist and how they might unintentionally perpetuate them. This recognition is a step toward meaningful change, as it highlights areas where leaders can take action to create a more equitable environment.

John's journey began with a public acknowledgment during a company-wide town hall meeting. He stood before the employees and recognized that Apex Pharma had not done enough to foster an inclusive environment. This public admission was a pivotal moment; he had moved through awareness and acknowledgment to mark the beginning of a new era of accountability within the company.

Accountability involves setting measurable goals and standards for DEI and being transparent about progress. John knew that accountability required more than just words of acknowledgment. It demanded concrete actions and measurable outcomes. He formed a DEI task force composed of diverse employees from various departments and levels within the company. This task force was empowered to audit the company's policies, practices, and culture, and to recommend specific, actionable changes.

One of the task force's first initiatives was to implement a comprehensive DEI training program for all employees, including the executive team. John participated fully, setting an example from the top. The training sessions were eye-opening, revealing unconscious biases and systemic barriers that many employees, including John, had not previously recognized. To ensure ongoing accountability, John instituted a system of regular progress reports. This transparency was key to maintaining momentum and building trust among employees. It also allowed for the identification of areas where progress was lagging, prompting timely interventions.

As John's progress reports demonstrate, accountability is about creating mechanisms for feedback and learning. Leaders must be open to hearing from those who are affected by their decisions, particularly from marginalized groups. This means actively soliciting feedback, listening without defensiveness, and being willing to make changes based on what they learn. By establishing channels for honest communication, leaders not only gain valuable insights into the effectiveness of their DEI efforts, but also show that they value and respect the perspectives of all employees. This openness fosters a culture of continuous improvement and reinforces the leader's commitment to DEI.

John worked with the compensation committee to tie executive bonuses and performance reviews to inclusion goals. This move underscored the company's commitment to DEI as a business imperative, not just a performative one. By holding himself and his peers on the leadership team accountable for achieving these goals, John demonstrated that DEI was integral to the company's success and sustainability.

However, accountability extends beyond organizational policies and structures. It requires personal accountability, where leaders must reflect on their own biases and behaviors. John committed to a personal journey of learning and growth. He engaged in regular self-assessment and sought feedback from colleagues, mentors, and DEI experts. By acknowledging his own blind spots and actively working to address them, John modeled personal accountability, demonstrating that DEI is not just an organizational goal but a personal commitment.

Moreover, accountability requires leaders to model the behaviors they wish to see in others. White male leaders must demonstrate a personal commitment to DEI through their actions, not just their words. This might include participating in DEI training, challenging their own biases, and speaking out against discrimination and inequity whenever they encounter it. By consistently modeling inclusive behavior, leaders set a powerful example for their organization, showing that DEI is a priority that everyone must uphold.

As these initiatives took root, the culture at Apex Pharma began to shift. Employees from diverse backgrounds felt more seen, heard, and valued. Innovation flourished as a wider array of perspectives and ideas were brought to the table. The company's reputation improved, attracting top talent who wanted to be part of an organization genuinely committed to DEI.

Lastly, accountability strengthens the organizational fabric by promoting trust and collaboration. When leaders hold themselves accountable, they build a foundation of trust that enables all employees to feel safe, respected, and valued. This trust is essential for fostering collaboration and innovation, as it encourages individuals to bring their full selves to work and to contribute their unique perspectives and ideas. A culture of accountability also ensures that everyone is held to the same standards, which reinforces fairness and equity throughout the organization.

John's journey illustrates that accountability is not about blame or guilt; it's about responsibility and action. For leaders, particularly white male leaders, it means using their influence to create equitable systems and environments where all employees can thrive. Accountability drives DEI forward by transforming intentions into impact, fostering trust, and ensuring that progress is sustained over the long term.

Through both organizational and personal accountability, leaders can drive meaningful change, build trust, and create an environment where inclusion is truly valued and upheld. This not only benefits the individuals within the organization but also enhances the overall effectiveness and resilience of the organization itself.

INCLUSIVE LEADERSHIP AT A GLANCE

Hold yourself and others accountable for fostering an inclusive environment.

Set clear goals and metrics for diversity and inclusion within your organization. Regularly review these goals and ensure that everyone, including yourself, is held accountable for meeting them. This might involve implementing training programs, revising policies, or promoting diverse voices within the leadership team. Additionally, create an environment where team members feel comfortable and safe in holding you and others to account. Encourage open dialogue and provide mechanisms for feedback, ensuring that concerns about inclusivity can be raised and addressed without fear of reprisal. This culture of mutual accountability is essential for continuous improvement and genuine inclusivity.

Building a Culture of Accountability

In today's highly connected and social environment, corporations are more susceptible to outside accountability than ever before in history. Corporate leaders can no longer get away with ticking boxes and putting out shiny reports void of any substance because the modern consumer expects much more. In response, many companies have begun opening themselves up to greater accountability in more meaningful and substantive ways. For instance, it's now just as common to see regular DEI reporting as it is to see a company's annual financial reports. This level of transparency allows the public and stakeholders to hold these companies accountable for what they are doing, or not doing, to drive DEI.

Another major accountability development is the integration of diversity metrics into executive compensation packages, as John did with his company. This means that a CEO's bonus might now depend on hitting specific goals related to increasing workforce diversity. By linking pay to performance, corporations send a strong message that DEI issues are just as important as financial ones.

Some companies turn to third-party audits and certifications as a method of accountability. Having an external party verify their claims adds credibility and ensures that companies aren't just paying lip service to DEI issues. It's like getting a stamp of approval that says, "Yes, we're doing what we say we're doing."

Starbucks gave a lesson in this type of accountability following a 2018 incident where two Black men were arrested while waiting for a friend.[1] The incident, which sparked widespread outrage and accusations of racial profiling, prompted Starbucks to close over eight thousand stores across the United States for one day to conduct racial bias training for its employees. This unprecedented move provided approximately 175,000 employees with education and skill-building around recognizing unconscious biases, understanding the impact of discrimination, and promoting a more inclusive and respectful environment within Starbucks stores. Developed in collaboration with experts and civil rights leaders, the curriculum included discussions on the history of civil rights, personal reflections, and group activities aimed at fostering empathy and understanding.

In addition to the training, Starbucks implemented new policies and procedures to ensure that similar incidents do not occur in the future, including its "Third Place Policy," which clarifies that everyone is welcome to use Starbucks spaces, whether they make a purchase or not.[2] It was a strategy designed to make Starbucks locations inclusive community hubs where everyone feels safe and respected. The company also established the "Civil Rights Assessment," an annual review conducted by external experts to assess the company's progress and help leadership identify areas for improvement and hold itself accountable to its commitments. By taking these comprehensive measures, Starbucks made a long-term commitment to corporate accountability, aiming to rebuild trust with its customers and communities.

Public commitments can also be highly effective at maintaining a level of accountability. When companies make public statements about improving diversity and inclusion, they create a sense of accountability and expectation as stakeholders watch to see if companies are walking the walk. Unilever, the parent company of iconic brands like Dove, has been at the forefront of inviting public accountability while making significant strides to address social inequalities. One of the company's most notable actions was their decision to remove the word "normal" from all beauty and personal care products and advertising. An aspect of Dove's "Real Beauty" campaign, which began in 2004, the public initiative challenged narrow beauty ideals and fostered a more inclusive and diverse representation of beauty throughout the marketplace.[3] The company stopped using terminology that marginalizes and excludes communities while also making substantial investments in diversity and inclusion programs. Unilever also set very public and ambitious targets to increase the representation of underrepresented groups in their workforce, particularly within leadership roles.

Taking their accountability efforts a step further, Unilever launched the Unstereotype Alliance, a coalition of companies and organizations working to eliminate harmful stereotypes in advertising.[4] This global initiative uses advertising to promote diverse and inclusive portrayals of people. Through these efforts, Unilever is not only demonstrating awareness and acknowledging its historical role in perpetuating societal biases within the beauty industry, the company is also actively working to dismantle those wrongs by setting a more responsible precedent for the industry.

In 2017, Dove released a Facebook advertisement featuring a Black woman removing her shirt to reveal a white woman underneath, followed by the white woman removing her shirt to reveal an Asian woman.[5] Some viewers critiqued the ad as a suggestion that lighter skin is preferable or that Dove's products "cleanse" darker skin to make it lighter. The widespread backlash included many references to Dove's perceived failure to follow its own public commitments. Critics argued that the ad was a tone-deaf mistake, particularly for a brand that had built its image around inclusivity and diversity.

Dove quickly pulled the ad and issued a formal apology, acknowledging that they had missed the mark and apologizing for any offense it caused. Dove and Unilever reiterated its commitment to representing all women, and reportedly took steps to prevent similar issues in the future by implementing more rigorous internal review processes for ads, particularly around sensitive topics such as race and diversity. This is a perfect example of how public initiatives and declarations can drive corporate accountability.

Final Thought: Accountability as a Path to Trust

It's uncomfortable to be held accountable for mistakes, but if we do this correctly, it prevents small issues from becoming larger ones. I have worked with too many organizations that have gotten themselves into complex legal issues because they did not adequately address small problems at their inception. Their leaders and managers had continuously let the daily microaggressions and seemingly small inequities slide, only to have the company end up as a defendant in a class action lawsuit because a group of former and current employees got together, and by sharing notes, realized that they were being discriminated against. Had leadership taken care of the issues early on by having the tougher, uncomfortable, but smaller conversations, they could have avoided a complex and expensive legal issue.

Accountability, I've learned, is not something I've had to demonstrate only once. It's an ongoing practice, woven into both my personal and professional life. Whether it's my daughters calling me out on a misstep or ensuring that my team's DEI efforts are implemented with care and attention, accountability is about being held to a standard, owning mistakes, and taking tangible actions to ensure they are not repeated.

Accountability is a path to trust because it demonstrates reliability, integrity, and a commitment to inclusion. When leaders hold themselves and others accountable for their actions, especially in promoting an inclusive environment, they show a dedication to fairness, consistency, and valuing diverse perspectives, which builds confidence among their teams. By taking responsibility for mistakes, addressing gaps, and ensuring that everyone has equitable opportunities to contribute and succeed, leaders foster a culture of transparency and belonging where trust can thrive. Accountability isn't about blame; it's about creating an environment where everyone knows that their contributions and experiences are valued, and where actions align with stated values. This alignment, coupled with a focus on inclusive practices, is foundational to earning and maintaining trust.

Ultimately, accountability is the bridge between intention and impact. It translates awareness, acknowledgement, and atonement into practical action. It's what transforms well-meaning efforts into meaningful change that deserves to be amplified. And while it's often uncomfortable and sometimes humbling, it's essential for growth—both for myself and the teams I lead. Through accountability, I've learned that the work of DEI is never truly done, but by holding myself to account, I can help create the structures and practices that move us toward a more inclusive future.

Tools to Build Accountability

Something You Can Do Right Now
Personal Accountability Journal: Begin a personal accountability journal dedicated to tracking your daily actions and decisions related to DEI. Use this journal to reflect on your interactions, choices, and behaviors throughout the day. Note instances where you demonstrated accountability and areas where you could improve. For example, consider whether you actively listened to diverse perspectives, challenged biased comments, or made inclusive decisions. Regularly reviewing your journal entries can help you recognize patterns, celebrate progress, and identify specific actions to enhance your accountability in fostering an inclusive environment.

Something You Can Do This Week
Accountability Partnerships: Establish accountability partnerships with a colleague or team member. Pair up with someone who shares your commitment to DEI and set specific, measurable goals related to diversity, equity, and inclusion for the week. These goals could range from attending a DEI training session to implementing a more inclusive meeting structure. Check in with each other regularly to discuss progress, share insights, and reflect on challenges. Hold each other accountable for achieving these goals and provide constructive feedback to support each other's growth. This partnership can help you stay focused and motivated while fostering a culture of mutual accountability within your organization.

Something You Can Do This Month

DEI Audit: Conduct a comprehensive DEI audit of your organization's policies, practices, and systems. This audit involves reviewing various aspects of your workplace, such as recruitment processes, promotion criteria, training programs, and employee feedback mechanisms, to identify areas lacking accountability structures. Collaborate with relevant stakeholders, including HR, DEI committees, and leadership, to gather data and insights. Once you've identified gaps, work together to develop and implement changes that enhance accountability. This might include establishing clear DEI goals, creating metrics for tracking progress, and setting up regular reviews to ensure ongoing commitment. By conducting a DEI audit, you can create a more transparent, accountable, and equitable workplace.

Chapter 8

Amplification

LIFTING OTHERS: USING PRIVILEGE TO EMPOWER AND ADVOCATE

"When leaders amplify diverse voices, they foster a culture where innovation thrives and everyone feels valued."

UNKNOWN

"When we amplify the best within us, we can achieve something miraculous."

BRENDON BURCHARD

Using My Voice for Others

Amplification. In my DEI journey as a white man, this concept has become one of the most important and empowering tools I've come to understand. While awareness, acknowledgment, atonement, and accountability have been vital to my personal growth, amplification marks a crucial shift from inward reflection to outward action—actively elevating the voices of those who are often unheard and ensuring their perspectives are not just included, but prioritized.

As I progressed in my DEI work, I realized that one of the most impactful things I could do was help create space for others, particularly those from marginalized communities, to have their ideas and experiences recognized. I had often been in meetings and decision-making spaces where I was one of the few people speaking, not because others didn't have valuable input, but because the environment wasn't structured to listen to them. I came to understand that my role wasn't just about speaking less—it was about amplifying the voices of others in a way that shifted the power dynamic.

One of the pivotal moments in my discovery of amplification came during a leadership meeting where we were discussing a new initiative focused on workplace culture. The conversation, as often happened, was dominated by a few voices—mostly those in leadership roles. One of my colleagues, a woman of color, had been trying to contribute to the discussion but was continually interrupted or overlooked. It was a pattern that I had witnessed numerous times before where a person comes into a meeting super engaged and ready to contribute, but their efforts to lean in are continuously overlooked by the majority presence in the room. As a result, they eventually retreat and stop attempting to engage altogether. When I noticed the woman fidgeting and sitting further back in her seat, I could sense her frustration was building. I also knew that the other leaders in the room had not tracked her demeanor, which is a common misstep for a lot of male leaders.

Given the work that I do, noticing these dynamics has become more natural to me. I don't think that is necessarily the case for most white men. It goes back to the white male culture of getting your point across, even if it means talking over someone else. Let me be clear though. There are many people from historically marginalized groups in the professional space who confidently jump right in and make their point, but there are also those who

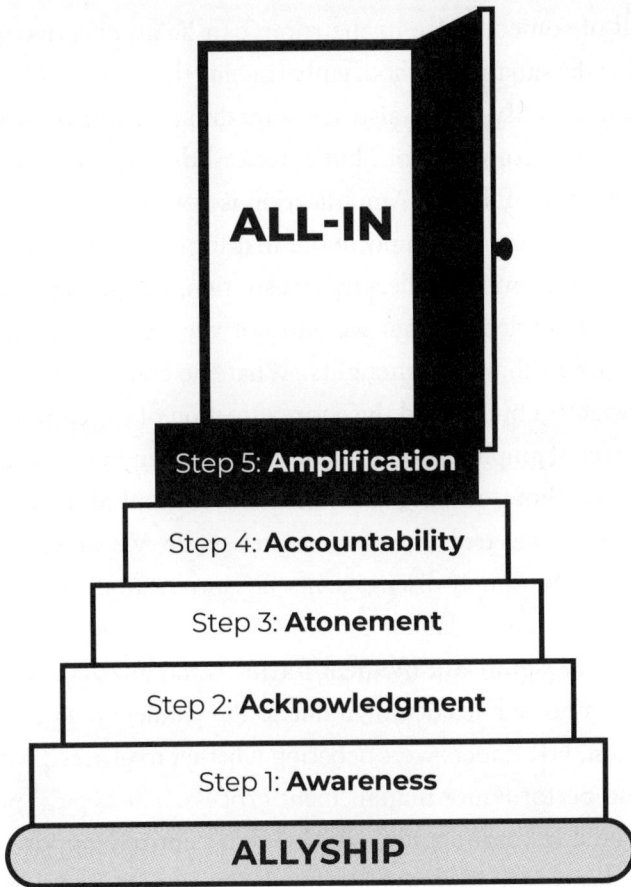

experience difficulty when trying to get their voices into the room, particularly for the first time. That's where the opportunity for amplification lies.

One of the subtle ways I try to do this is by placing the blame on myself. I may say something like, "Oh, I'm sorry, Jose. I think you were starting to talk, and I jumped in. Can you share what you were going to say?" I've found that putting the responsibility on me instead of someone else in the room can be an effective way of handling the situation without embarrassing the person whose voice I want to amplify. I may also say something like, "I want to add something in conversation, but I noticed that Theresa has been trying to jump in here." Amplification is not about making some grandiose gesture. It's simply about making space for all voices.

Upon noticing my colleague's frustration, I stopped the conversation, acknowledged that we had not yet heard from her, and invited her to share her thoughts. What she contributed was not only insightful but shifted the entire direction of the conversation. The power of amplification became clear to me in that moment—it wasn't just about offering someone the floor, but about ensuring that the floor was truly theirs when they spoke. We were fortunate that she did not simply disengage in that conversation, which would have been understandable.

Another significant moment for me came in 2020, when the world was turned upside down due to the pandemic. In a lengthy discussion, HR leaders were debating whether to proceed with our year-end performance management process. The typical process was rooted in meritocracy, which I don't entirely oppose when executed correctly. However, during that unprecedented time, I felt strongly that continuing with the process as usual was simply wrong. I could see that most of the burden of caretaking, home-schooling, and managing life was falling on women, who were balancing these responsibilities while also holding down full-time jobs from home. The idea of continuing with the normal process, without acknowledging this reality, didn't sit well with me.

Instead of staying silent, I took the calculated risk of speaking up. I argued that we should adopt a less stringent and more equitable approach, at least for that year, in an effort to recognize the unique challenges faced by many of our employees. To my amazement, after the meeting, several of my female colleagues reached out privately to thank me for speaking up. They expressed that while they had felt the same way, they were uncomfortable putting voice to the sentiment in that setting. I realized that the "risk" I had taken was not that risky for me at all. But for others it would have been too risky for them to call it out. Although we ended up sticking with the normal process, this experience drove home the power of leveraging my privilege to amplify the voices of others who may not feel empowered to do so.

In developing this aspect of the framework, I came across two definitions of amplification that I found particularly informative. The first definition is: "to increase the volume or intensity." The second one is: "material added to a story in order to expand or clarify it." Within the All-In Framework, amplification at its best is a combination of these two definitions. As I have pointed out throughout this book, the advancement of the DEI conversation has stalled due in part to the absence of amplification by white male leaders. By highlighting the work of historically underrepresented groups, we not only acknowledge the valuable efforts of the people who have been in this fight for decades, but we also challenge ourselves to carry the ball further down the field.

I've witnessed this scenario unfold countless times. For instance, I'll make a statement about advancing representation in the leadership ranks to a group of white male leaders, with one non-white or non-male diversity leader present. After sharing my thoughts or recommendations, I often see the men nodding in agreement, as though they're hearing the concept for the first time, while the diverse leader displays a look of complete exasperation. Because I already recognize the source of that frustration, I make a point to ask these diverse leaders how many times they have communicated the same or similar information to the group, and the answer is always some iteration of "dozens of times." This is what happens when amplification is missing from white male leadership.

Amplification is not just a passive act of giving space in the moment; it's about using my voice to advocate for those who need it, pushing for changes in systems and policies that have historically marginalized certain groups. It's an active process that requires intentionality and a commitment to change. It's about encouraging white men to use our platforms and influence to highlight diverse experiences and push for structural shifts in how organizations operate. I began to see my role as an amplifier not just in meetings, but in all aspects of my work. Whether it was in project planning, decision-making, or hiring, I recognized that I had the ability—and responsibility—to use my platform to ensure that underrepresented voices were not only heard but valued. Amplification became a form of allyship that allowed me to step back while lifting others up. It's not just about saying, "I support DEI," but about actively showing that support by amplifying the voices of those who have been excluded from the conversation for too long.

Amplification in Action

Charles, a seasoned financial services executive known for his strategic acumen, was faced with an unprecedented challenge—massive numbers of diverse employees exiting the organization. As a leader, he recognized the need to navigate the complex landscape of DEI with more than just good intentions. He realized that embracing and driving DEI efforts couldn't just be something to cross off his list if he wanted to reverse the attrition trend; it required a fundamental shift in both perspective and practice. This realization marked the beginning of his journey to understand and implement the critical principle of amplification.

For Charles, this meant using his influential position to ensure that the contributions and ideas of marginalized groups were not only heard but valued and acted upon. He also recognized that the need for white men to take a more active role in the DEI conversation was equally crucial.

There is a bit of courage that goes along with amplifying voices because it can be uncomfortable. Charles began by focusing on creating visibility for underrepresented groups with the understanding that making their contributions visible to the entire organization was crucial for dismantling stereotypes and biases. Deliberate actions to highlight the work and ideas of diverse employees in meetings, newsletters, and other communication channels showcased the immense value these perspectives brought to the table. By amplifying historically underrepresented voices, Charles began to harness the full range of creativity and problem-solving abilities within his team.

Consistently amplifying diverse voices also built trust between Charles and his employees. It demonstrated his genuine commitment to DEI, encouraging all employees to engage more fully and authentically with their work. This trust was further solidified by creating platforms such as forums, panels, and committees where diverse voices could influence strategy and decision-making.

Mentorship and sponsorship were vastly expanded, with senior leaders actively working with individuals from underrepresented groups and helping them advance within the organization. This effort ensured that diverse voices were heard at higher levels, further embedding DEI principles into the fabric of the company. Additionally, leadership encouraged feedback from diverse employees and took concrete actions based on their insights and suggestions, strengthening the culture of amplification.

Recognizing the pivotal role white men play in advancing DEI, Charles took steps to amplify this need within his leadership circles. He organized workshops and discussions specifically targeted at white male leaders, emphasizing their responsibility in fostering an inclusive environment. These platforms became essential to addressing common misconceptions and biases, encouraging his peers to become active leaders in the DEI journey. By openly discussing the unique position of influence that white male leaders hold, Charles highlighted the necessity for them to lead by example and champion DEI initiatives with conviction.

Through these efforts, Charles ensured that amplification helped hold the organization accountable for its DEI commitments. Amplification naturally follows accountability when DEI is pursued sincerely. By making diverse contributions more visible, it became easier to track progress and identify areas needing further effort. Charles held a strong belief that amplifying historically underrepresented groups is simply the right thing to do and leaders would get on board for that reason.

By moving beyond awareness and acknowledgment and actively amplifying diverse voices, Charles fostered a culture of inclusion that transformed his organization. One notable example was during an annual strategy meeting. Charles noticed that Maya, a junior analyst from a traditionally underrepresented background, had insightful ideas during team discussions but often hesitated to speak up in larger meetings. Determined to amplify her voice, Charles made it a point to invite her to present her innovative project proposal to the executive team. He also spent time with Maya prior to the meeting, offering to assist in whatever way she requested. Maya's presentation was a resounding success, leading to the implementation of her ideas across multiple projects. This not only boosted Maya's confidence and career trajectory but also set a powerful precedent for recognizing and promoting diverse talent.

Charles also championed the creation of a Diversity Council, composed of employees from various backgrounds and levels within the company. This council was given a significant role in shaping company policies, from recruitment to diversity suppliers to community engagement initiatives. Amplifying the voices within this council ensured that diverse perspectives were incorporated into the company's strategic decisions. The council's insights led to a more inclusive hiring process, which saw a notable increase in diversity across all levels of the organization.

Charles's efforts in amplification also extended beyond the company walls. Recognizing the impact of his efforts beyond the business case, he partnered with his Community Affairs team to forge partnerships with local schools and community organizations, creating mentorship programs that connected company employees with diverse youth. These programs not only provided valuable opportunities and guidance for the next generation but also enriched the company's culture by fostering a deeper understanding of the communities they served. But these efforts also provide a roadmap for leaders inside of organizations that are not particularly open to diversity amplification. Leaders can have an external voice outside of their company by looking toward the community for amplification opportunities.

Consistently, Charles sought to measure the impact of these initiatives. He implemented regular surveys and feedback loops to assess the effectiveness of amplification efforts and to identify areas for improvement. This data-driven approach ensured that the company's DEI strategies were not static but evolved based on real-time insights and employee experiences. Amplifying the voices of diverse employees is only part of the equation. For DEI efforts to truly take root, it is essential for white male leaders to actively participate, set an example, and initiate a ripple effect throughout the organization that encourages other leaders and managers to take similar actions. The power of amplification is transformative. When leaders commit to elevating every voice, they unlock the true potential of their organizations.

INCLUSIVE LEADERSHIP AT A GLANCE

Use your platform to amplify marginalized voices and advocate for DEI efforts.

Inclusive leaders use their influence to elevate those who may not have the same visibility or opportunities. Actively promote and support the work of individuals from underrepresented groups. This could mean advocating for their ideas, providing them with opportunities to lead projects, or mentoring them for advancement. Furthermore, take a more active role in highlighting and advocating for DEI efforts within your organization and industry. By championing these initiatives and encouraging other leaders to do the same, you help create a more equitable and diverse workplace, setting a standard for others to follow.

Amplifying Underrepresented Voices

Ice cream giant Ben & Jerry's offers an example of the power of externally amplifying the voices of historically underrepresented communities. With decades of proven advocacy, the company has established itself as unwavering in the fight for social justice, consistently utilizing its extensive platform to amplify voices around racial equity, LGBTQ+ rights, and environmental justice. Its bold "Dismantle White Supremacy" campaign served as a call to action for policy reform and drove uncomfortable, yet necessary, conversations around the racial inequalities that are entrenched within our society.[1] They routinely partner with racial advocacy groups, offering the invaluable resource of their vast audience to highlight their efforts.

Ben & Jerry's has also consistently advocated for LGBTQ+ rights, amplifying the fight for marriage equality long before the Supreme Court acted upon it. Their support for environmental justice is also effectively loud and unrelenting. From their supply chains to their ice cream containers, Ben & Jerry's amplifies the cause of sustainable practices and environmental policies that prioritize the well-being of marginalized communities disproportionately affected by environmental degradation. These actions demonstrate the power of corporate social responsibility in advocating for systemic change and amplifying the voices of marginalized communities. Ben & Jerry's has positioned itself as a leader in social justice advocacy within the corporate world and among consumers, setting a precedent for other companies to follow.

Nike is another major corporation that prioritizes the amplification of marginalized voices across its platforms. Internally, the company has implemented programs to increase representation at all levels, including the board of directors and executive leadership positions to ensure the amplification of these voices in decision-making processes and product development. Externally, Nike participates in numerous community partnerships and empowerment programs with a focus toward youth development, education, and sports participation in underserved communities. With the launch of initiatives like the "Equality" campaign which featured athletes like Serena Williams and LeBron James,[2] and their iconic "Just Do It" campaign which has featured people of different races, ethnicities, genders, religions, ages, and abilities, Nike has amplified messages of equality that resonates with audiences globally. Even with the controversy that has accompanied some of their social justice efforts, the company ranks as the world's largest seller of athletic footwear, apparel, and equipment.

Many of today's consumers hold corporations to a moral obligation of advancing human rights and social justice both within their walls and the larger society. As a result, the amplification of marginalized voices has become an imperative for building trust and credibility among stakeholders, including customers, investors, and local communities. Internal and external amplification, done with intention and coupled with active involvement from all leaders, especially white men, can foster a truly inclusive and thriving environment.

Final Thought: The Ripple Effect

One of the most rewarding aspects of amplification is seeing the long-term impact it can have. I've seen colleagues, whose voices were once overlooked, grow in confidence and leadership skills when given the chance to truly contribute. In some cases, they've become the ones to amplify others, creating a ripple effect that expands beyond just one conversation or meeting.

Amplification is about power—how we use it and how we yield it. As a white man, I've come to understand that part of my privilege is having access to spaces that others might not. By amplifying others, I'm not giving away my power, but rather redistributing it in ways that make our organizations, teams, and communities stronger. It's about ensuring that the voices of those who have been marginalized are no longer pushed to the edges but are central to the conversation.

I was not speaking for others. Instead, I was ensuring that those who needed to be heard had the space, opportunity, and support to speak for themselves. It's a practice that demands both awareness and action, and one that has allowed me to shift from focusing on my own role in DEI to empowering those around me. Amplification is a continuous, active process that encourages white men to use their platforms not only to elevate diverse voices but to advocate for systemic change—moving beyond individual conversations toward creating sustainable, equitable environments for all.

Tools for Amplification

Something You Can Do Right Now

Self-Reflection Exercise: Take a moment to engage in a self-reflection exercise focused on amplification. Reflect on the voices you hear most often in your workplace and consider whose voices might be missing or undervalued. Write down a list of colleagues whose contributions you find valuable but may not always receive the recognition they deserve. Contemplate how you can amplify these voices in meetings, discussions, and decision-making processes. Consider how you might encourage other leaders, especially white men, to speak on the work they are doing to engage in DEI efforts. By recognizing whose voices need amplification as well as demonstrating your willingness to be vocal, you can start to foster a more inclusive environment.

Something You Can Do This Week

Amplification Sessions: Schedule one-on-one meetings with team members whose voices you want to amplify. During these sessions, actively listen to their ideas and feedback. Acknowledge their contributions and express your intent to support them. Ask open-ended questions to better understand their perspectives and challenges. Following these sessions, look for opportunities in meetings and collaborative projects to echo their ideas and give them credit. By doing this, you help to elevate their voices and demonstrate your commitment to a more inclusive workplace.

Something You Can Do This Month

Amplification Workshop: Collaborate with HR or DEI specialists to organize a workshop focused on the concept of amplification. Bring together employees from across the organization to discuss the importance of amplifying underrepresented voices. Share examples of successful amplification and its positive impact on team dynamics and innovation. Facilitate open dialogue and encourage participants to share their experiences and strategies for amplification. By hosting this workshop, you create a platform for employees to learn how to effectively amplify others, fostering a culture where everyone's voice is valued and heard.

Chapter 9

WHY ALL-IN MATTERS

"When you go all in, you forget about the 'what ifs,'
the doubts, and the fear. You're left with purpose,
and that drives everything else."

UNKNOWN

In the Flow

For me, going All-In means a relentless dedication to this work—continuously learning, challenging my own biases, and using the platforms I have to make a tangible impact. I've seen firsthand how crucial it is, especially for leaders like myself—white, male, and in positions of influence—to actively engage in shaping more equitable environments. I've watched too many well-meaning leaders stumble, unsure of how to have meaningful conversations about race, gender, privilege, and systemic inequality. I've experienced those same challenges myself, often unsure of what to say or how to show up in difficult moments.

But in those moments, I began to understand that the silence of people like me—whether out of discomfort or fear of saying the wrong thing—was perpetuating the very systems we hoped to dismantle. I knew I couldn't stand on the sidelines anymore. I had to go deeper. I had to move from being an observer to becoming an active participant in driving change. That's why I do this work. Not because I have all the answers, but because I believe that doing nothing is no longer a viable answer.

Going All-In is not about perfection; it's about persistence and the willingness to keep showing up, even when it's hard. Being All-In is about having an appreciation for my privilege and for the opportunities that come from that privilege. It's about changing the white male narrative around privilege from a place of guilt or shame to that of a recognition that privilege is a commodity, a commodity that we are wasting due to our lack of appreciation. We can use our privilege to create opportunities for connection and relationship. We can use our privilege to help build someone up and to help open the eyes of other white men in positions of power and influence. Being All-In is necessary work and I believe that together, we can create something better—something truly inclusive for everyone.

Being All-In on DEI efforts means reaching a level of engagement where inclusive practices become an intrinsic part of how you and the organization operate. It's not about ticking boxes or following a script; it's about embodying inclusivity in every action and decision, almost without thinking. This state offers profound benefits, transforming not just individual leadership but the entire organizational culture.

When you are All-In, proactive advocacy becomes a natural extension of your role. You find yourself speaking up in meetings to ensure diverse perspectives are heard, not out of obligation, but because it feels like the right thing to do. Redirecting conversations to include input from underrepresented voices or challenging decisions that overlook equity concerns becomes second nature. You're no longer waiting for a moment to intervene, you're actively shaping discussions to be more inclusive from the start.

When you're All-In, inclusion as part of decision-making happens effortlessly. Planning an event? You automatically consider accessibility, diverse representation, and inclusive language, embedding these elements into the process without even pausing to think of them as separate tasks. They're simply a part of how decisions are made, ensuring that inclusivity isn't an afterthought but a fundamental criterion.

This flow state also means you have the ability to recognize and act on bias immediately. You don't need to rehearse or prepare how you'll respond to microaggressions or stereotypes when they arise; you address them calmly and constructively in the moment. Whether it's offering support to someone affected by bias or calling out inappropriate comments, you do so without blaming and shaming but with confidence that comes from having internalized these values.

Mentoring and sponsorship become more than just duties, they become a seamless part of your professional routine. You instinctively look for opportunities to mentor or sponsor individuals from marginalized groups. It's not about fulfilling a DEI quota—it's about leveraging your influence to amplify others' work, nominate them for projects, and provide them with platforms to showcase their skills. These actions flow naturally from a mindset that recognizes the importance of contributions from a diverse set of voices.

The journey of going All-In also involves continuous self-reflection and learning. It's not a static state but a dynamic process of growth. You habitually engage in self-reflection, seek feedback, read, and learn about diverse experiences. This ongoing learning integrates seamlessly into how you lead and interact with others, allowing you to adapt and evolve in your inclusion efforts.

When it comes to building inclusive teams, you naturally prioritize diversity and representation. Whether hiring or forming project groups, you automatically seek out candidates with varied backgrounds and perspectives. You understand that diverse teams lead to richer discussions and more innovative solutions, and you compose these teams instinctively, knowing that inclusivity drives better outcomes.

Inclusive communication becomes an ingrained habit. You use gender-neutral terms effortlessly, actively listen, and structure meetings in ways that allow everyone to contribute comfortably. It's not a matter of remembering to be inclusive, it's simply how you communicate, ensuring that every voice feels valued and heard.

Finally, being in this flow means embedding DEI into the organizational culture without it feeling forced. DEI isn't a separate initiative to manage—it's woven into the fabric of everyday practices. You integrate DEI goals into performance metrics, recognize and reward inclusive behaviors, and lead by example. In doing so, you help create an environment where everyone is encouraged to bring their whole selves to work.

Being All-In on DEI means that your efforts no longer feel performative or forced. They are embedded in how you lead, work, and interact daily. When you reach this state, the benefits are clear: a more inclusive, dynamic, and equitable workplace where diversity isn't just acknowledged, it's celebrated and leveraged for collective success.

Finding My All-In Flow

I can recall a moment when I realized I was truly "in the flow" of being All-In on DEI efforts. It was during a strategic planning session with my team. The agenda was packed—goal setting, planning, deadlines, budgets—but as we delved into the conversation, I noticed that the focus on inclusivity and diverse perspectives came effortlessly, almost as if it was embedded into the foundation of our discussion. The ideas and energy were flowing.

One of my team members was presenting a proposal for a benefits vendor. Traditionally, we might have jumped straight into risks, issues, and financial projections. But this time, without thinking, I found myself asking questions about how we had ensured a range of perspectives in the selection process. I wanted to know whose voices had been included in the focus groups, whether we had considered the accessibility of the product, and how our new vendor would resonate with diverse communities. These questions weren't scripted or part of a formal checklist—they simply flowed from an ingrained understanding that inclusion is integral to success.

As the meeting progressed, it was clear that the team had adopted this mindset too. We discussed how to incorporate feedback from diverse employees, not as a separate DEI initiative, but as a core part of our strategy. One of my colleagues, who had previously been more reserved on these topics, confidently suggested collaborating with an employee resource group to better understand the needs of underrepresented groups. This was a moment that felt different—more organic. It was as if we had collectively moved past the phase of "trying to be inclusive" and into a space where inclusivity was just how we operated.

Later that day, a team member approached me to express their appreciation. They shared that our conversations had become noticeably more inclusive over time, and it made her feel valued and heard. That feedback was a turning point. It made me realize that being All-In on DEI wasn't necessarily about grand gestures or formal declarations. It was about those subtle, natural shifts in how we conducted our daily business.

In that flow state, I wasn't merely fulfilling my role as an advocate—I was living it. I didn't need to remind myself to amplify others' voices or think twice about challenging biases—they were instinctive actions. Being All-In had become a part of who I was as a leader, shaping not just my decisions but the culture around me. It was then that I understood: when you're truly in the flow, All-In isn't something you do—it's a state of mind, a way of being, and an integral part of who you are.

Ally to All-In Framework in Action

Bill was a relatively new, internally appointed leader within a large telecommunications company. The organization brought me in as a leadership consultant to help Bill set up his management routines as well as establish a productive team culture. While observing a leadership meeting, I watched Bill—an executive with a previously strong advocacy for diversity and inclusion—inadvertently display behaviors that contradicted his stated values. Throughout the meeting Bill repeatedly interrupted and spoke over Tina, the head of the finance team. His pattern of interaction was not only limited to Tina but seemed to be a broader issue affecting the entire dynamic of the predominantly white male leadership team. This interaction offered a potentially pivotal moment of self-discovery and growth for Bill to begin his journey through the Ally to All-In model.

Bill would have described himself as an ally who supported DEI efforts. He prided himself on his commitment to fostering an inclusive environment and believed he was doing his part to champion diversity and inclusion within the organization. However, the events that unfolded revealed that there was a significant gap between his intentions and his actions. Recognizing the opportunity for a teachable moment, I scheduled a one-on-one meeting with Bill to address these observations. Armed with examples and a clear plan to invoke reflection and change, I approached the discussion with candor and sensitivity. I described my observations as factually as possible along with my assessment of how his behavior may be hindering the team culture. Bill, initially taken aback by the feedback, displayed a range of emotions from defensiveness to introspection. However, his genuine commitment to his principles soon took over, paving the way for a constructive dialogue.

This meeting marked Bill's first step into the Awareness stage, where he confronted the discrepancy between his actions and his values. The discomfort he felt was essential. It served as the catalyst for his journey toward becoming a truly inclusive leader.

As we progressed to the Acknowledgment phase, Bill took the step of not only internalizing the feedback but also planning to address it directly with Tina. This was a significant move that involved him openly admitting his shortcomings in a subsequent meeting with her. By stating, "I have been made aware of my tendency to interrupt you in meetings, and I want to acknowledge this with you," he initiated a vulnerable and honest conversation. This acknowledgment was crucial for setting the stage for genuine change and served to validate Tina's experiences, fostering a new level of trust between them.

Moving into Atonement, Bill expressed a sincere apology to Tina, specifying the behaviors he intended to change and discussing the broader implications of his actions. He committed to a series of steps designed to not only improve his interactions with Tina but also to serve as a role model for the rest of the team. This included actively practicing better listening skills, encouraging open dialogue, not tolerating this behavior in other leaders, and facilitating a space where all voices could be equally heard and valued.

Accountability took shape through Bill's proactive approach to ensuring that his behaviors aligned with his values. He set up a system with other team members where they could openly provide feedback if they noticed any recurrence of the problematic behaviors. This not only helped Bill stay on track but also encouraged a culture of openness and mutual accountability among the leadership team.

Finally, the Amplification stage saw Bill leveraging his position to advocate for broader cultural changes within the organization. He began using his influence to promote diversity and inclusion initiatives, ensuring that such topics were prioritized in every business agenda. Bill also started to highlight the contributions of underrepresented groups within the company, actively seeking to elevate voices that had previously been marginalized. Equally as important, he began to share the process he had been through, and continued to go through, in the hope that other leaders could also learn.

Through this journey Bill transformed from a leader who merely supported diversity and inclusion in theory to one who actively embodied these principles in his daily actions. Initially, he saw himself as an ally to DEI efforts, believing that his support was sufficient. However, over time, Bill demonstrated that he could go All-In and become a more inclusive leader. This shift not only enhanced his professional relationships but also significantly impacted the company's culture, making it more inclusive and equitable. The ripple effects of his actions demonstrated the profound impact that a commitment to true change could have, not just within a team, but across an entire organization.

The Reversal Risk

In 2024, Tractor Supply Company announced a decision to abandon its diversity policies and efforts, including the elimination of all DEI roles and the discontinuation of support for Pride events.[1] This sharp reversal from the company's previously lauded inclusive practices is only one example of a broader trend where major companies have scaled back or abandoned DEI programs due to public and political scrutiny. Beer manufacturer Molson Coors Beverage Co. sent an employee memo stating its intention to end a policy linking executive compensation to employee representation. The company also terminated its supplier diversity goals, and ended its participation in the Human Rights Campaign's corporate rankings. Automotive manufacturer Ford Motor Company, though being listed among the US's and Mexico's best places to work for LGBT equality in 2017, also made the decision to stop its participation in the index.[2,3]

One of the most startling retreats from DEI policies came from tech giant Google. Widely seen as a longtime pioneer and leader within the diversity space, the company significantly scaled back its initiatives in 2024, cutting back on its DEI staff and programs. In 2020, Google took center stage as one of the most prominent corporate voices to champion the benefits and importance of diversity and inclusion. Its leadership pledged to increase the number of underrepresented groups in leadership roles and to specifically double the representation of Black employees among non-senior positions by the year 2025. But by 2023, Google abandoned many of its DEI goals, citing economic challenges and the tech sector's slowdown.[4] The company did away with roles that focused on the recruitment of underrepresented groups and significantly reduced internal programs around building a more inclusive workplace.

While this shift illustrates a growing narrative around DEI, there are still many major corporations going All-In on their diversity commitments and doubling down on their efforts in spite of the opposition. Beer company Heineken continues to emphasize DEI as a core aspect of its business strategy. With a focus on increasing gender equity within the organization, the company has made significant strides in gender representation among management roles, continuing its goal of having 30 percent of its leadership positions held by women.[5] Beyond the internal policies, Heineken is also focused on advancing gender equity externally through financial partnerships with women-owned businesses and entrepreneurs, particularly in markets where access to capital for women is limited. The company has taken a holistic approach that not only aligns with its broader corporate social responsibility goals, but also its financial goals by creating and maintaining an environment that reflects its diverse customer base.

The active commitment of being All-In is as important as ever in today's corporate space, even as we see some companies moving backward. This work is not going away, nor should it. The next generation of workers will demand diversity and inclusion as part of the work culture, but so will an increasing number of stakeholders, as we have seen with companies like Goldman Sachs. The investment and financial services corporation recently faced pressure from its shareholders to better align its diverse practices with its public commitments. The coalition of activist groups and investors called public attention to perceived discrepancies between the company's stated advocacy for diversity and its actual actions, arguing that Goldman Sachs falls short of its promises on key DEI issues.[6] This pushback exemplifies the potential consequences when organizational leaders fail to align DEI efforts with the core values and operations of the company. Yes, true integration should be reflected in HR policies like recruitment practices, performance evaluations, and promotion criteria. But it should also show up in the professional actions of leaders and decision-makers. Oftentimes, especially within the corporate world, what gets measured is what gets done. But being All-In is about the long game, not solely short-term play. Companies that bow to the pressure of a social media campaign or the comfort of maintaining the status quo of inequity are being shortsighted and putting themselves at future risk from a business perspective.

There is a reason why successful companies like PepsiCo, Salesforce, and Costco continuously embrace diversity initiatives in the face of opposition. They understand the value that it brings to the promotion of sustainability and better financial outcomes. These leaders see DEI as both morally and strategically imperative to the futures of their organizations. PepsiCo's Self-ID LGBTQ+ program allows employees to voluntarily disclose their sexual orientation, gender identity, or other diversity attributes in a confidential manner.[7] The company then analyzes the provided data to help leaders better understand the composition of its workforce and better provide resources for its LGBTQ+ employees. The information is also used to track progress on LGBTQ+ inclusion, ensure equitable

opportunities for advancement, and provide necessary accommoda-
tions, such as gender-neutral facilities. This is the type of diversity
policy that goes All-In by actively acknowledging and addressing
potential disparities in the workplace, while also amplifying the
voices of underrepresented groups.

Salesforce is known as one of the most successful contact management software companies on the market, and it is also known
as a trailblazer in addressing systemic issues like the gender pay gap
and underrepresentation in the workforce. The company has strategically aligned its DEI initiatives with its corporate culture, investing millions to ensure pay parity across its workforce.[8] Salesforce's
diversity strategy includes increasing the number of underrepresented employees in leadership roles and creating opportunities for
career advancement through mentorship and training programs.
Leadership also created programs offering comprehensive benefits
to transgender employees and the company consistently supports
global Pride events.

Costco has demonstrated a steadfast commitment to diversity,
equity, and inclusion, even as some companies face pressure to pull
back. In early 2025, Costco shareholders overwhelmingly rejected
a proposal to evaluate potential risks tied to the company's DEI
practices—over 98 percent voted against it, signaling strong internal support.[9] This commitment appears to resonate with customers:
Costco gained nearly 7.7 million shopping trips in just four weeks
following Target's rollback of its DEI programs, with notable
increases among Black and Hispanic/Latino households.[10] Finan-
cially, the company continues to thrive, reporting a 7.5 percent
increase in sales and a 13 percent rise in net income over the previous year, with its stock outperforming the S&P 500.[11] Costco's

example reinforces the message that leading with inclusion can align with both values and business success.

It is our responsibility as All-In advocates to ensure that we are pushing back against efforts to pull back or reverse DEI initiatives. We must actively engage in advocating for progress, not allowing complacency or backlash to undermine the gains made. This means using our voices, influence, and positions of power to challenge decisions or behaviors that threaten to stall or regress DEI efforts. We need to encourage the organizations we work for and have influence within to go All-In on their support for DEI, recognizing that the journey is ongoing and requires sustained commitment.

Moreover, our advocacy shouldn't stop at our workplaces. As consumers of goods and services, we have power in where we choose to spend our money and which companies we support. We should encourage these organizations to stay the course, publicly demand accountability for their DEI commitments, and reward those that prioritize inclusion and equity. By aligning our values as consumers with our actions as advocates, we can amplify our impact, making it clear that DEI is not a trend but an enduring, essential practice for a fair and thriving economy and society.

A FINAL NOTE
ON THE PATH FORWARD

In 2020, America faced a profound reckoning ignited by the murder of George Floyd. This horrific event forced us as a society to confront the deep-seated inequities that have long been embedded within our institutions and daily lives. It was a moment that demanded more than just reflection; it required action. Companies across the nation responded swiftly, issuing statements of solidarity and launching initiatives aimed at promoting diversity, particularly for women and people of color. This was a long-overdue focus, one that finally brought much-needed attention to voices that had been marginalized for far too long.

Yet, amid the flurry of actions and the urgency to address these inequities, a crucial element was overlooked: the engagement of white men in DEI efforts. We were quick to launch programs, set metrics, and create executive roles dedicated to diversity. We looked for solutions that could be implemented, measured, and celebrated. But in our rush to fix what was broken, we missed a fundamental step. We failed to invite white men—those who have historically held positions of power and influence—to truly engage in this work on a personal level. We failed to ask them to pause, to reflect, and to be vulnerable.

In our haste, we overlooked the power of introspection. We didn't encourage white men to question their relationship with DEI, to explore how they experience their own race, gender, and sexual orientation, or to recognize the privileges they carry with them every day. We avoided the uncomfortable questions: When have I been complicit? Why have I been complicit? What do I stand for, and what kind of legacy do I want to leave behind? Without confronting these questions, we risk perpetuating the very systems we are trying to dismantle and being complicit in the backsliding of DEI progress.

As I look back on my journey, I realize that what started as a slow shift in perspective has become something much deeper—a commitment to go All-In for diversity, equity, and inclusion. Where I stand today is not just as an ally, but as someone fully invested in helping to create spaces where every person can thrive.

This is why I wrote *From Ally to All-In*. I wanted to give not only myself but other leaders, especially white male leaders, a pathway forward—something concrete to help them navigate the complexities of DEI work. This book isn't just about my own personal journey or those of a select few of the leaders I have worked with; it's a call to action for others who may feel stuck on the sidelines of allyship and unsure of how to move forward. I wanted to offer the tools and permission to be vulnerable that I wish I had had earlier to help other leaders move from passive awareness to active, committed engagement.

This book is a plea to change the current narrative around DEI. It's an invitation for everyone, but particularly for white men, to move beyond superficial commitments and go deeper, to step out of our comfort zones, and to confront the realities of our own positions within these systems of inequality. We must pause, reflect, and ask ourselves the tough questions about who we are and what we want our contributions to this world to be. This is not about blame or guilt; it's about acknowledging our roles and using our influence to foster change.

I believe, deeply and fundamentally, that all people share common desires: to be accepted, loved, understood, seen, and valued. Over the years, my journey—from standing in the "White Men" quadrant, shocked by the clear expectation that I should be leading DEI, to now being invigorated by the challenge—has revealed the incredible potential for transformation within each of us. This potential extends beyond creating better workplaces; it's about reinventing how we interact with each other and with the world at large. It's about creating a society where everyone has the opportunity to thrive, free from the constraints of systemic bias and discrimination.

How will we know where the finish line is? When will this work be done? These are not questions for me, as a white man, to answer or declare. The ultimate measure of success lies in the eyes of the beholder—those who have been marginalized, overlooked, or discriminated against. It is their experiences and perspectives that will guide us. We must follow their lead in defining what true equity and inclusion look like, and until they feel accepted, loved, understood, seen, and valued, our work continues.

So, where am I now? I'm still learning, still evolving, and still making mistakes along the way. But I'm also fully committed to this journey, and I've embraced the responsibility that comes with it.

To my fellow white men: we stand at a unique threshold, a moment in history where we have the power to effect meaningful change. We have the opportunity to cast aside outdated roles and narratives, to transition from a place of privilege to a place of purpose. We can use our influence not to preserve the status quo, but to help usher in a kinder, more equitable future. This is not just about fulfilling a corporate initiative or checking off a box; this is about redefining who we are and what we stand for.

A better future is possible—one where inclusivity is not just an ideal, but a lived reality for all. However, this future can only be realized if we, especially those of us who have been afforded privilege, have the courage to step up and help lead the charge. It requires us to engage fully, to be willing to make mistakes, and to learn and grow from them. It calls for an ongoing commitment to awareness, acknowledgment, atonement, accountability, and amplification of the voices that have been silenced for too long, including our own.

As I close this book, I want to leave you not with a sense of conclusion, but with a sense of beginning. This is not the end of a journey, but the start of a lifelong commitment to driving change. I'm not just hopeful; I'm resolute. I am committed to going All-In—to challenging myself and others to create spaces where every individual can be accepted, loved, understood, seen, and valued. This work is not easy, nor is it ever truly finished, but it is necessary. It's time to step up—not just for ourselves, but for the generations to come, for a future that holds the promise of equity and belonging for all.

Let's go All-In, together.

SELF-ASSESSMENT GUIDE FOR THE ALLY TO ALL-IN FRAMEWORK

Introduction

This self-assessment tool is designed to help leaders gauge their current standing in their journey toward being inclusive. Each section corresponds to a stage in the Ally to All-In Framework, with reflective questions and practical actions to help you deepen your engagement.

1. Awareness

Awareness is the first step, where you begin to recognize inequities, systemic biases, and your role within them.

Reflection Questions

- How aware am I of the systemic privileges and disadvantages that exist within my workplace and society?
- Do I actively seek to understand the lived experiences of people from marginalized groups?
- Can I identify moments when I have witnessed or unintentionally participated in exclusionary behaviors or systems?

Rating (1-5)

1 = Not at all aware.

5 = Deeply aware and seeking more understanding.

Total:

Next Steps

- Make it a habit to read, listen, and learn from diverse voices, whether through books, podcasts, or conversations.
- Attend DEI training, if available, or seek out educational resources on systemic inequity.

2. Acknowledgment

Acknowledgment involves recognizing how privilege and systemic issues have shaped your worldview and how they continue to impact marginalized groups.

Reflection Questions

- Have I acknowledged my own privilege and identity and the ways it has benefited me, especially in professional settings?
- How comfortable am I with having conversations about race, gender, and other forms of identity?
- When confronted with uncomfortable truths about inequity, how do I react?

Rating (1-5)

1 = I haven't acknowledged my privilege.
5 = I regularly acknowledge privilege in discussions and actions.

Total:

Next Steps

- Begin or continue to have open conversations about privilege, identity, and inequity, starting with your team.
- Reflect on how you can use your position of influence to create more equitable environments.

3. Atonement

Atonement is about taking responsibility for past actions or inactions that contributed to inequality and making amends.

Reflection Questions

- Have I taken responsibility for times when I may have unintentionally perpetuated bias or inequity?
- Am I actively seeking to make amends by correcting past actions or speaking up when I see inequity now?
- Have I apologized for times when my words or actions caused harm, even unintentionally?

Rating (1-5)

1 = I've not yet acknowledged past mistakes.
5 = I actively seek to repair harm and learn from past behavior.

Total:

Next Steps

- Apologize when necessary, especially if you've realized past behaviors or decisions were harmful.
- Engage in restorative conversations where you listen to those impacted and take actions that demonstrate commitment to change.

4. Accountability

Accountability is about ensuring that you and others are held responsible for creating inclusive environments and taking meaningful action.

Reflection Questions

- Do I regularly hold myself accountable for fostering inclusivity and equity in my professional and personal life?
- How often do I check in with my team, peers, or even family to ask for feedback on how I'm doing in this area?
- Am I open to receiving feedback, especially when it challenges my perspective?

Rating (1-5)

1 = I rarely hold myself accountable.
5 = I consistently hold myself and others accountable, welcoming feedback.

Total:

Next Steps

- Set measurable goals for inclusivity and regularly track your progress.
- Create a circle of accountability—colleagues or mentors who will give you honest feedback about your inclusivity efforts.

5. Amplification

Amplification means using your influence to lift up marginalized voices and advocate for systemic change.

Reflection Questions

- How often do I use my platform to highlight the achievements and experiences of underrepresented colleagues?
- Do I advocate for systemic change in my organization or industry to create a more inclusive culture?
- Am I proactive about creating opportunities for diverse voices to be heard?

Rating (1-5)

1 = I rarely amplify diverse voices.
5 = I regularly use my platform to amplify underrepresented voices and advocate for systemic change.

> **Total:**

Next Steps

- Commit to actively mentoring and sponsoring individuals from underrepresented backgrounds.
- Advocate for policies in your organization that promote inclusivity, such as gender-neutral restrooms, flexible working hours, or diverse hiring practices.

> **Total Score:**

Here's how to interpret your results:

Assessment Scoring Scale

After completing the assessment, tally up the points from each section. Your total score will give you an idea of where you stand on the *Ally to All-In* journey.

0-35 Points: Back to Chapter 1

Uh-oh! It seems like you're still figuring things out. You may have taken the first step, but there's more work to be done. Time to roll up your sleeves, go back to the basics, and revisit some core concepts of awareness and acknowledgment.

- **Next Steps:** Dive deeper into DEI resources, engage in tough conversations, and start building a stronger foundation. It's never too late to learn more and improve.

36-50 Points: Comfortably in Allyship

You've made some progress and are comfortable in your role as an ally. But comfort can sometimes mean complacency. There's more you can do to actively engage in making change. You're on your way, but don't settle here!

- **Next Steps:** Push yourself out of your comfort zone. Seek more opportunities to hold yourself accountable and amplify others. Keep learning, growing, and stretching beyond what feels easy.

51-65 Points: Moving in the Right Direction

Look at you! You're definitely moving in the right direction, and people are noticing. You've got a solid understanding of allyship, and you're starting to take real action. You're well on your way to being a strong advocate and amplifying the voices of those who need it most.

- **Next Steps:** Keep that momentum going! Focus on accountability and amplification—use your platform to create lasting change. You're making great strides, but there's always more room for impact.

66-75 Points: Go Amplify!

Wow, you're on fire! You've shown exceptional commitment to going All-In, taking meaningful actions at every stage of the Ally to All-In Framework. You're a leader who amplifies marginalized voices and advocates for systemic change. Keep it up—there's no limit to the positive impact you can make!

- **Next Steps:** Stay humble, keep listening, and remember that allyship is a lifelong journey. Use your influence to mentor others and lead the way in creating more inclusive environments.

Bonus

For those who score **75 points: All-In!**

You are the embodiment of All-In—you've fully embraced the journey of inclusive leadership, and you're making a significant difference. Your peers see you as a true ally and champion for equity. Now, go out there and keep amplifying!

Final Thoughts

Take time to reflect on your scores. What stage do you feel strongest in? Where do you see room for growth? This assessment is not meant to be a judgment but a guide to help you on your path to becoming a more engaged and effective ally. Progressing through the Ally to All-In Framework is an ongoing journey that requires continuous learning, reflection, and action.

By being intentional in each of these steps, you can become a stronger advocate for equity, diversity, and inclusion in all areas of your life.

360° ASSESSMENT TOOL FOR THE ALLY TO ALL-IN FRAMEWORK

Introduction

This 360° assessment tool is designed to facilitate feedback between colleagues on their inclusivity journey by gathering feedback from managers, direct reports, and peers. The following sections align with the five stages of the Ally to All-In Framework: Awareness, Acknowledgment, Atonement, Accountability, and Amplification. This tool is intended to foster honest and constructive discussions, helping each other grow as inclusive leaders.

360° Feedback Guidelines

- Be honest yet constructive in your feedback, highlighting both strengths and areas for improvement.
- Ensure feedback is specific, citing examples and offering actionable suggestions.
- Approach the feedback process with a spirit of collaboration, aiming to help your colleague grow in their allyship journey.

1. Awareness

Feedback on the leader's awareness of inequity, systemic bias, and their role in addressing it.

Reflection Questions

- Does this leader demonstrate awareness of systemic inequities and biases within the organization or broader society?
- Do they actively seek to understand diverse perspectives and lived experiences?
- Have they demonstrated growth in their awareness over time?

Rating (1-5)

1 = Shows little awareness.
5 = Consistently demonstrates a deep awareness of systemic issues.

Total:

Comments

- Provide specific examples of how this person has shown (or not shown) awareness of inequity and bias.

Suggestions for Improvement

- Offer ideas on how they can increase their awareness of systemic inequities and biases.

2. Acknowledgment

Feedback on how effectively the leader acknowledges privilege and engages in difficult conversations.

Reflection Questions

- Does this leader recognize and openly acknowledge their own privilege, particularly in discussions around race, gender, and equity?
- Are they comfortable and proactive in having challenging conversations about identity and bias?
- Have they admitted when their perspective or actions might have been shaped by privilege?

Rating (1-5)

1 = Does not acknowledge privilege or engage in difficult conversations.
5 = Regularly acknowledges privilege and seeks difficult conversations.

Total:

Comments

- Provide examples where the leader has effectively acknowledged privilege or areas where they could improve.

Suggestions for Improvement

- How can they create more space for discussions about privilege and inequity in the workplace?

3. Atonement

Feedback on whether the leader takes responsibility for past actions or inactions and seeks to repair harm.

Reflection Questions

- Has this leader taken responsibility for any past actions or inactions that may have contributed to inequity?
- Are they proactive in addressing past missteps and making amends when necessary?
- Do they demonstrate humility and a willingness to learn from mistakes?

Rating (1-5)

1 = Rarely takes responsibility for past actions.
5 = Consistently takes responsibility and seeks to repair harm.

Total:

Comments

- Provide examples of how the leader has atoned for past mistakes or discuss areas where they have been less effective.

Suggestions for Improvement

- Offer thoughts on how they can take more responsibility for fostering a more inclusive environment.

4. Accountability

Feedback on how well the leader holds themselves and others accountable for inclusive practices.

Reflection Questions

- Does this leader hold themselves accountable for their role in creating an inclusive environment?
- Do they create spaces where feedback on inclusivity is welcomed and acted upon?
- Have they taken specific actions to hold others accountable when they see bias or exclusion?

Rating (1-5)
1 = Rarely holds self or others accountable.
5 = Regularly holds self and others accountable for inclusivity.

Total:

Comments

- Give examples where this leader has demonstrated (or not demonstrated) accountability for inclusivity.

Suggestions for Improvement

- Share ways in which they can strengthen accountability, both for themselves and others.

5. Amplification

Feedback on whether the leader uses their platform to elevate marginalized voices and advocate for systemic change.

Reflection Questions

- Does this leader actively seek to amplify underrepresented voices in meetings, decision-making, or strategic discussions?
- Have they used their position of influence to advocate for systemic change or create new opportunities for diverse voices?
- Do they mentor or sponsor individuals from underrepresented backgrounds?

Rating (1-5)

1 = Rarely amplifies diverse voices.
5 = Consistently amplifies voices and advocates for systemic change.

Total:

Comments

- Share examples where the leader has used their platform to amplify diverse voices, or provide feedback on how they could improve.

Suggestions for Improvement:

- Recommend ways they could further use their influence to advocate for underrepresented groups or systemic changes.

Total Score:

Here's how to interpret your score:

360° Assessment Scoring Scale

After your colleagues complete the assessment, total the points across all categories. This score will give you an idea of how your colleagues view your allyship efforts.

0-35 Points: Lost in Translation

Hmm, your colleagues are seeing some gaps in your allyship journey. Maybe your good intentions aren't always landing or being communicated clearly. It's time to revisit some foundational allyship practices and re-engage with those around you.

- **Next Steps:** Ask for more specific feedback and be open to learning. Reconnect with your colleagues, listen actively, and take steps to bridge the gap between your intentions and actions.

36-50 Points: Ally in the Making

You're getting there! Your colleagues see that you've started on your allyship journey and are comfortable engaging, but there's room for growth. You're doing well, but now's the time to take that allyship up a notch.

- **Next Steps:** Challenge yourself to go deeper in areas like atonement and accountability. Be more proactive in engaging your colleagues and advocating for change. You're on the right path—just keep moving forward!

51-65 Points: Respected Ally

Your colleagues appreciate your efforts, and they see you as a trusted ally who's committed to making a difference. You've got a solid foundation, and your actions are speaking louder than words. Your peers are noticing your contributions.

- **Next Steps:** Keep focusing on amplification—use your platform to elevate marginalized voices. You're already making an impact, but there's always more to do. Push yourself to hold others accountable and lead by example.

66-75 Points: Amplification Master

Wow! Your colleagues see you as a leader who walks the walk when it comes to allyship. You're not just talking about DEI, you're living it in everything you do. You're amplifying voices, holding yourself and others accountable, and making systemic change.

- **Next Steps:** Keep up the momentum and continue being a role model. Share your allyship journey with others and help guide them along the path. Remember, allyship is a continuous process, so keep learning and growing.

Bonus for those who score 75 Points: All-In and Winning

Your colleagues think you're doing an outstanding job! You've fully embraced the Ally to All-In Framework, and your actions reflect it. They see you as a genuine champion of inclusivity and equity. Congratulations!

Final Thoughts

This 360° assessment provides valuable insights into how leaders are perceived on their Ally to All-In journey. The feedback should be delivered constructively, focusing on encouraging growth and development rather than critique. Once the feedback is received, leaders should take time to reflect and incorporate the suggestions into their leadership approach.

GOING ALL-IN ON INCLUSIVE LEADERSHIP: A LEADER'S CHEAT SHEET

This cheat sheet is designed to serve as a quick reference guide for leaders committed to inclusive leadership within their organizations. It outlines practical actions and strategies to help leaders move from passive allyship to active, All-In involvement in fostering an inclusive environment.

1. Self-Reflect

- Regularly examine your biases and stereotypes.
- Interrupt biased thoughts and actions in real-time.
- Participate in unconscious bias training.

2. Educate Yourself

- Diversify your reading list with diverse authors.
- Attend DEI workshops and training sessions.
- Follow and engage with diverse voices online.

3. Promote Inclusivity

- Advocate for inclusive policies in your workplace.
- Seek diverse input when making decisions.
- Use inclusive language in all communications.

4. Participate in DEI Initiatives

- Join or support Employee Resource Groups (ERGs).
- Volunteer for DEI-related projects.
- Push for policies that support diversity and inclusion.

5. Take Responsibility

- Reflect on your own privilege and its impact.
- Advocate for policy and procedural changes that promote equality.
- Hold yourself accountable for aligning actions with equity principles.

6. Listen and Amplify Voices

- Create safe spaces for open conversations.
- Ensure underrepresented voices are heard in meetings.

- Use your privilege to amplify marginalized voices.

7. Be an Accomplice

- Educate others about underrepresented groups' experiences.
- Speak up against injustice and bias.
- Offer mentorship and sponsorship to underrepresented individuals.

How to Use It

- **Daily Reminder:** Keep this cheat sheet accessible (e.g., on your desk or as a digital note) to serve as a daily reminder of the key actions you can take to actively support DEI efforts.
- **Self-Assessment:** Use it to periodically assess your progress and identify areas where you can deepen your commitment. Reflect on which actions you are already taking and which ones you can incorporate into your routine.
- **Guide for Conversations:** Leverage this tool during discussions with your team or peers about DEI initiatives, using it as a framework to guide conversations and encourage collective action.
- **Team Meetings:** Incorporate this cheat sheet into team and department meetings as a concise guide for leaders seeking practical ways to go All-In on DEI.
- **Action Planning:** Use the outlined activities as a starting point for creating a personal or team action plan focused on building a more inclusive environment.

NOTES

A Note for Straight White Male Leaders

1 "Products - Data Briefs - Number 206 - June 2015." 2019. www.cdc.gov.
   June 7, 2019. https://www.cdc.gov/nchs/products/databriefs/db206.htm.

2 "KSHB: Suicide Rates High in Middle-Aged White Men." n.d. Saint Luke's
   Health System. https://www.saintlukeskc.org/about/news/
   kshb-suicide-rates-high-middle-aged-white-men.

3 Statista. 2018. "U.S.: Mass Shootings by Race 1982-2018 | Statista." https://
   www.statista.com/statistics/476456/
   mass-shootings-in-the-us-by-shooter-s-race/.

4 "Why Are Mass Shooters Overwhelmingly White Men? - North Shore."
   n.d. https://digitaledition.chicagotribune.com/tribune/article_popover.
   aspx?guid=62ba50e8-ae08-4ab6-bdf1-e4e46b6e9b1b.

A Note for Leaders Representing Historically Marginalized Communities

1 "Products - Data Briefs - Number 206 - June 2015." 2019. www.cdc.gov.
   June 7, 2019. https://www.cdc.gov/nchs/products/databriefs/db206.
   htm.

2   "KSHB: Suicide Rates High in Middle-Aged White Men." n.d. Saint Luke's Health System. https://www.saintlukeskc.org/about/news/kshb-suicide-rates-high-middle-aged-white-men.

Chapter 1

1   *Inclusive Leadership Transforming Diverse Lives, Workplaces, and Societies,* edited by Bernardo M. Ferdman, Jeanine Prime, and Ronald E. Riggio, 2021. Pgs. 363-366, Routledge.
2   Ibid.
3   Ibid.

Chapter 3

1   Lorenzo, Rocío, Nicole Voigt, Miki Tsusaka, Matt Krentz, and Katie Abouzahr. 2018. "How Diverse Leadership Teams Boost Innovation." BCG Global. January 23, 2018. https://www.bcg.com/publications/2018/how-diverse-leadership-teams-boost-innovation.
2   Carucci, Ron. 2024. "One More Time: Why Diversity Leads to Better Team Performance." *Forbes.* January 24, 2024. https://www.forbes.com/sites/roncarucci/2024/01/24/.one-more-time-why-diversity-leads-to-better-team-performance/.
3   "Harvard Business Publishing Education." 2024. Harvard.edu. https://hbsp.harvard.edu/product/H03IGV-PDF-ENG.
4   Hunt, Dame Vivian, Lareina Yee, Sara Prince, and Sundiatu Dixon-Fyle. 2018. "Delivering Growth through Diversity in the Workplace." www.mckinsey.com. McKinsey. January 18, 2018. https://www.mckinsey.com/capabilities/people-and-organizational-performance/our-insights/delivering-through-diversity.
5   Ibid.
6   "Statistics on Diversity, Equity and Inclusion - Inclusive Outcomes." 2018. Inclusive Outcomes. October 18, 2018. https://www.inclusiveoutcomes.com/the-stats/.
7   Saulsbery, Gabrielle. 2022. "A Case for Diversity." UPSTATE BUSINESS JOURNAL. June 3, 2022. https://upstatebusinessjournal.com/business-news/the-case-for-diversity/.

Chapter 5

1   BBC. 2018. "Uber Investigated over Gender Discrimination." BBC News, July 16, 2018. https://www.bbc.com/news/business-44852852.

2   Juran, Katie. 2018. "Opportunity for All." Adobe.com. https://blog.adobe.
     com/en/publish/2021/03/24/opportunity-for-all?scid=1605f3ec-22bc-4551-
     8561-5c6df50cfe5b&mv=social&mv2=owned_social.

3   Kochhar, Rakesh. 2023. "The Enduring Grip of the Gender Pay Gap." Pew
     Research Center. March 1, 2023. https://www.pewresearch.org/social-
     trends/2023/03/01/the-enduring-grip-of-the-gender-pay-gap/.

4   Ibid.

5   Ibid.

6   Ibid.

7   Ibid.

8   Schwartz, Matthew S. 2019. "Google Pay Study Finds It Underpaid Men for
     Some Jobs." NPR, March 5, 2019, sec. Technology. https://www.npr.
     org/2019/03/05/700288695/google-pay-study-finds-its-underpaying-
     men-for-some-jobs.

9   Villarreal, Daniel. n.d. "Victoria's Secret CEO Resigns Following
     Transphobic Comments." LGBTQ Nation. https://www.lgbtqnation.
     com/2018/11/victorias-secret-ceo-resigns-following-transphobic-comments/.

10   Flanagan, Hanna. 2020. "Victoria's Secret Launches Its Most Diverse Ad
     Campaign Featuring Transgender and Curvy Models." PEOPLE.com.
     March 20, 2020. https://people.com/style/victorias-secret-launches-diverse-
     campaign-with-transgender-curvy-models/.

Chapter 6

1   "Target Commits to Spending More than $2 Billion with Black-Owned
     Businesses by 2025." n.d. Corporate.target.com. https://corporate.target.
     com/press/release/2021/04/target-commits-to-spending-more-than-
     2-billion-wit.

2   "Procter & Gamble 'Take on Race' Fund Supports Black Americans." 2020.
     Global Cosmetic Industry. June 5, 2020. https://www.gcimagazine.com/
     brands-products/news/news/21860972/
     procter-gamble-take-on-race-fund-supports-black-americans.

3   Little, Becky. 2020. "How a New Deal Housing Program Enforced
     Segregation." HISTORY. October 20, 2020. https://www.history.com/
     news/housing-segregation-new-deal-program.

4   The United States Department of Justice. 2023. "The Fair Housing Act."
     Justice.gov. U.S. Department of Justice. https://www.justice.gov/crt/
     fair-housing-act-1.

5   "JPMorgan Chase Commits $30 Billion to Advance Racial Equity." n.d. Www.jpmorganchase.com. https://www.jpmorganchase.com/ir/news/2020/jpmc-commits-30-billion-to-advance-racial-equity.

6   "Wells Fargo Launches $400 Million Small Business Recovery Effort." 2020. Wf.com. https://newsroom.wf.com/English/news-releases/news-release-details/2020/Wells-Fargo-Launches-400-Million-Small-Business-Recovery-Effort/default.aspx.

7   Editors, History.com. 2018. "Negro League Baseball." HISTORY. A&E Television Networks. August 21, 2018. https://www.history.com/topics/sports/negro-league-baseball.

8   "MLB Recognizes Negro Leagues as 'Major League' — Correcting a 'Longtime Oversight.'" n.d. NPR.org. https://www.npr.org/2020/12/16/947226542/mlb-corrects-longtime-oversight-now-recognizes-negro-league-as-major-league.

9   MLB.com. 2024. "The Most Encouraging Performances of the Season for Each Team." MLB.com. MLB. September 12, 2024. https://www.mlb.com/news/mlb-players-who-took-biggest-steps-forward-2024?msockid=2c8d8e0a8d9d6bb029d89f948c996a15.

Chapter 7

1   Abbas, Tahir. 2023. "Navigating the Storm: Starbucks Crisis Management Case Study." CMI. June 5, 2023. https://changemanagementinsight.com/starbucks-crisis-management-case-study/.

2   Ibid.

3   Sharadha, R. 2020. "An Analysis of Dove's Breakthrough Marketing Campaign, 'Real Beauty.'" Hustle Monk. September 3, 2020. https://medium.com/hustle-monk/doves-breakthrough-marketing-campaign-involved-empowerment-of-real-women-ad2734c0188a.

4   Unilever PLC. 2023. "Unstereotype 101 Guide: How to Speak out against Stereotypes." July 14, 2023. https://www.unilever.com/news/news-search/2023/unstereotype-101-guide-how-to-speak-out-against-stereotypes/.

5   "Dove Apologizes after Backlash over Ad." 2017. AP News. October 10, 2017. https://apnews.com/article/business-media-social-media-race-and-ethnicity-african-americans-7ac7ed7bd88148bea3e49962bbb0d6e3.

Chapter 8

1   Silence Is NOT an Option." n.d. https://www.benjerry.com/home/about-us/media-center/dismantle-white-supremacy.

2   Monllos, Kristina. 2017. "Nike Just Released a Gorgeous, Powerful Campaign Dedicated to Equality." Adweek.com. Adweek. February 12, 2017. https://www.adweek.com/brand-marketing/nike-just-released-a-gorgeous-powerful-campaign-dedicated-to-equality/.

Chapter 9

1   Treisman, Rachel. 2024. "Tractor Supply Slashes Its DEI and Climate Goals after a Right-Wing Pressure Campaign." NPR. June 28, 2024. https://www.npr.org/2024/06/28/nx-s1-5022816/tractor-supply-dei-climate-backlash.

2   "Ford Listed among Best Places to Work for LGBT Equality in U.S. And Mexico | Ford Media Center." 2017. Ford.com. https://media.ford.com/content/fordmedia/fna/us/en/news/2017/12/11/ford-listed-among-best-places-to-work-for-lgbt-equality-in-u-s--.html.

3   Guynn, Jessica. 2024. "Ford Becomes Latest High-Profile American Company to Pump Brakes on DEI." *USA TODAY*. August 28, 2024. https://www.usatoday.com/story/money/2024/08/28/dei-backlash-hits-ford/74982898007/.

4   Moreno, Johan. 2023. "Google Slashes Diversity Programs after Big Promises." *Forbes*. December 31, 2023. https://www.forbes.com/sites/johanmoreno/2023/12/31/google-slashes-diversity-programs-after-big-promises/.

5   Perez-Chao, Fernando Alonso, and Elisabeth Pipic. 2024. "These Organizations Are Getting Corporate Diversity, Equity and Inclusion (DEI) Right." World Economic Forum. January 8, 2024. https://www.weforum.org/agenda/2024/01/organizations-impactful-corporate-dei-initiatives/.

6   Segal, Mark. 2021. "Goldman Sachs Raises Diversity Expectations for Corporate Boards." ESG Today. December 2, 2021. https://www.esgtoday.com/goldman-sachs-raises-diversity-expectations-for-corporate-boards/.

7   Birch, Kate. 2024. "How PepsiCo's Data-Driven Approach Advances Diversity and Inclusion Goals." Sustainabilitymag.com. February 2, 2024. https://sustainabilitymag.com/diversity-and-inclusion-dandi/pepsicos-data-driven-approach-to-diversity-and-inclusion.

8   Perez-Chao, Fernando Alonso, and Elisabeth Pipic. 2024. "These Organizations Are Getting Corporate Diversity, Equity and Inclusion (DEI) Right." World Economic Forum. January 8, 2024. https://www.weforum.org/agenda/2024/01/organizations-impactful-corporate-dei-initiatives/.

9   Tabassum, Juveria, and Kerber, Ross. 2025. "Costco Shareholders Reject Call For Review of Diversity Programs." Reuters. January 23, 2025. https://www.reuters.com/business/retail-consumer/costco-shareholders-vote-against-proposal-report-diversity-programs-2025-01-23/.

10   Reuter, Dominick.2025. "Costco Is Looking Like the Big Winner After
        Target's DEI Rollback." Business Insider. March 12, 2025. https://www.
        businessinsider.com/shoppers-ditching-target-choosing-costco-after-
        dei-shift-2025-3.
11   CBS/AP. 2025. "Costco Shareholders Reject Anti-DEI Measure, After
        Walmart and Others End Diversity Programs." CBS News. January 24,
        2025. https://www.cbsnews.com/news/costco-dei-policy-board-statement-
        shareholder-meeting-vote/?utm_source=chatgpt.com.

ACKNOWLEDGMENTS

Writing this book has been a deeply personal and rewarding journey, and it would not have been possible without the support and guidance of so many remarkable people.

To my daughters, Kylie and Cameron, thank you for continually inspiring me to strive for a better, more inclusive world. Your generation and the ones behind you hold the torch for the future, and I am proud to learn from you every day.

I want to express my deepest gratitude to my family, especially Tracy, whose unwavering support and encouragement have carried me through the challenging and fulfilling moments of this process. Your patience and belief in me have been a great source of strength.

A heartfelt thanks goes to my friends and colleagues who have supported me in this endeavor. Thank you for your insights, your honest feedback, and for walking this journey alongside me. I am grateful for your commitment to inclusivity and for challenging me to think more deeply and to act with greater purpose.

To my clients, past and present, who have trusted me with your stories, struggles, and triumphs—you have provided the real-world context that shaped much of the content of this book. Your courage and willingness to engage in difficult conversations continue to inspire me.

I want to offer special thanks to my book coach, Erika Winston. Your expertise, encouragement, and belief in this project helped shape it into what it is today. You guided me through every tantrum and draft, offering invaluable wisdom and helping me stay on course. I couldn't have reached this point without your support.

To the Amplify Publishing Group, especially Will Wolfslau, Myles Schrag, J.C. Heins, and Josh Taggert, thank you for your unwavering support, guidance, and expertise in bringing this book to life—your dedication made this journey not only possible but deeply rewarding.

Finally, to the countless voices, mentors, and thought leaders in the diversity, equity, and inclusion space—thank you for laying the foundation for this work. Your tireless efforts continue to shape the path forward, and I am honored to be a part of this movement.

This book is dedicated to everyone who believes in the power of change, growth, and inclusivity. It is my hope that the words within these pages contribute to the ongoing dialogue for a more equitable and just world.

Thank you.

ABOUT THE AUTHOR

M ike Lynch is a seasoned coach, facilitator, and speaker with over thirty years of experience spanning corporate and non-profit sectors. Throughout his career, he has held a variety of leadership roles, including executive HR positions, where he has ignited growth, orchestrated transformation, and driven success for executives, leadership teams, and organizations.

Widely recognized as a "client whisperer," Mike is passionate about fostering inclusion and empowering leaders to meet transformative challenges. As the creator of the Ally to All-In Framework, Mike guides leaders—especially white men—on a journey from passive allyship to active, wholehearted engagement in building inclusive environments. With his ability to prompt leaders to view challenges through a fresh lens, embrace change, and develop new perspectives, Mike equips them with the clarity, self-awareness, and tools to become effective agents of change.

In 2023, Mike founded **MJL Consulting Group** to further his mission of inclusive leadership. Through his work, he encourages leaders to go beyond passive allyship and actively embrace diversity, equity, and inclusion (DEI) in meaningful ways. He partners with clients to create cultures that foster innovation, collaboration, and equity at every level.

When he's not guiding others on their leadership journey, Mike enjoys spending quality time with family and friends, exploring the outdoors, and pursuing his fitness goals. Based in Virginia, Mike is driven by a deep commitment to inclusion and growth, with a mission to inspire meaningful change—one conversation and one action at a time.

Mike can be reached at mike@mjlconsultinggroup.com.

SHARE *FROM ALLY TO ALL-IN* WITH LEADERS

If you found this book valuable and believe others in your network would benefit from it too, I encourage you to share it with fellow leaders, especially white male leaders. If you are considering purchasing the book for your team or entire organization, please reach out to **mike@mjlconsultinggroup.com** to inquire about bulk discounts.

WOULD YOU LIKE TO BRING *FROM ALLY TO ALL-IN* TO YOUR ORGANIZATION?

Mike offers a select number of speaking, workshop facilitation, and leadership coaching engagements each year, focusing on inclusive leadership. If you're interested in bringing his message to your organization, please contact **mike@mjlconsultinggroup.com** or visit **www.mjlconsultinggroup.com**.